Of Water and the Spirit:
Mission and the Baptismal Liturgy

Of Water and the Spirit: Mission and the Baptismal Liturgy

Phillip Tovey

First published in 2015 by the Canterbury Press Norwich
Editorial office
3rd Floor, Invicta House,
108–114 Golden Lane,
London EC1Y 0TG

Canterbury Press is an imprint of Hymns Ancient & Modern Ltd
(a registered charity)
13A Hellesdon Park Road, Norwich,
Norfolk, NR6 5DR, UK

www.canterburypress.co.uk

British Library Cataloguing in Publication data

A catalogue record for this book is available
from the British Library

978 1 84825 803 7

Typeset by Manila Typesetting Company

Printed and bound in Great Britain by
CPI Group (UK) Ltd, Croydon

Contents

List of Tables

Foreword

This book owes its inspiration to two things. The first was a book by E. C. Whitaker, *The Baptismal Liturgy*, which was very influential in my thinking when the *Alternative Service Book* came out.[1] It seemed to me that a similar book of relative short size might be helpful for those using *Common Worship*. The second factor is 20 years of teaching courses in the Diocese of Oxford for lay people and Reader candidates on baptism and confirmation, and then another ten years teaching ordinands at Ripon College Cuddesdon part time. In this period my thinking has gradually evolved, not least seeing the close connection between baptism and mission and the need for this to be stronger in our thinking. Mission courses often omit baptism altogether, and baptismal courses may view mission simply from the lens of people asking for their children to be baptized. Neither of these is very adequate, and both of these omit the missional shaping of the baptismal liturgy, and the baptismal liturgy shaping mission. My hope is that this book will go some way to bring these two things together and thus put baptism as a key part of mission action planning, rather than being relegated to a 'policy' separated from mission thinking. In one way the book is about the relationship of one of the five marks of mission to the others; but more about that later.

Terminology

I want to start by rejecting completely the notion of 'occasional offices' as including baptism. The language is now completely outmoded; baptism is a gospel sacrament, and *Common Worship* has pastoral rites – marriage, funerals, healing. It would be much better to use the terminology of sacrament and pastoral rites instead of occasional offices.

A similarly complex issue arrives with the use of 'Christian initiation', which I have tried to avoid. This is a slippery term and of relatively new provenance. Its use in part comes from an adaptation of Arnold van Gennep's classic *The Rites of Passage*, and seems to have been introduced by Louis Duchesne in his *Christian Worship*.[2] But we do not need to write rites of passage and there is not a 'sacrament of initiation'. We tell good news and administer baptism as our gospel work. I suggest a better term is 'rites of baptism', or 'baptismal rites' for ceremonies and symbols accompanying baptism (including confirmation and catechumenal rites). The debate about where some services should go, for example should thanksgiving for the birth of a child be in pastoral rites rather than initiation, is one that I have raised which has not been successfully concluded.

Acknowledgements

I want to thank Mark Earey for his many helpful suggestions in looking over the manuscript while in a busy term and Christine Smith for her encouragement in this project.

Notes

1 E. C. Whitaker, 1965, 1981, *The Baptismal Liturgy*, London: SPCK.

2 Arnold van Gennep, 1960, *The Rites of Passage*, Chicago: University of Chicago Press, and Louis Duchesne, 1904, *Christian Worship: Its Origin and Evolution*, 2nd edn, London: SPCK.

1

Baptism, Mission and the Roots of Baptismal Liturgy

Baptism is both the fruit of mission and a call to mission. This can be seen in the pages of the New Testament, from the baptism of Jesus to the baptisms in the book of Acts, and the discussion of baptism in the Epistles. (See Matt. 3.13–17; Mark 1.9–11; Luke 3.21–22; Acts 2.37–41; 8.14–17; 8.36–39; 9.17–19; 10.44–48; 16.13–15; 16.25–34; 19.1–7; Rom. 6.1–4; 1 Cor. 1.13–17; Eph. 4.3–6; Titus 3.3–8; Heb. 6.1–3; 1 Peter 3.18–22.) This chapter will look at the relationship between baptism and mission and the rudiments of baptismal liturgy in the New Testament and other early Christian literature. There are other major works that look into baptism in greater depth and the Notes and Bibliography should be consulted for further references: few discuss the intimate connection with mission.[1]

The baptism of Jesus and his mission

The baptism of Jesus inaugurates his mission. John baptizes in the desert region calling people to turn away from their sins, but he looks forward to the person who will baptize with the Holy Spirit. The baptism of Jesus transforms John's baptism of repentance with the revelatory event of the Triune God. The voice of the Father, the Son coming up from the river Jordan, and the Spirit descending as a dove reveals baptism in the Holy Trinity (Mark 1.9–11). It also shows Jesus as the first person baptized in the Holy Spirit, beginning the new age. The declaration of the voice of God 'You are my Son' establishes Jesus' unique position. The words spoken by the Father indicate the nature of the mission of Jesus. On the one hand 'You are my Son' is from Psalm 2.7 indicating royal authority, and on the other, 'who I love; with you I am well pleased' is from Isaiah 42.1, a passage about the servant of the Lord. Thus from his very baptism, Jesus is the one with authority but also the servant, and the two are united in his own person and in the way he conducts his mission.

After a time of preparation in the desert Jesus begins his ministry of preaching the kingdom of God (Matt. 4.1–11, 17). He becomes an itinerant evangelist, but soon calls together a team to work with him in his mission (Matt. 4.17–25). This mission has a number of elements to it, including preaching, healing and deliverance. The disciples are gradually drawn into this mission (Matt. 12). Thus the baptism of Jesus is an inauguration of the mission of the kingdom of God, which soon becomes the development of a 'little flock', whose calling is to be incorporated into that mission (Luke 12.32). From these early shoots of what is to become the Church, mission is the heartbeat of its life.

Jesus also saw the end of his life in terms of baptism: 'I have a baptism to undergo, and how distressed I am until it is completed!' (Luke 12.50). This is not an isolated statement. In Mark 10.38 Jesus says, 'Can you drink the cup I drink or be baptized with the baptism I am baptized with?' This is in reply to some of his disciples asking whether they will sit at his right hand in glory. The passage ends with Jesus reiterating the Son of Man coming to serve, clearly pointing back to the words at his baptism, and rightly seeing everything in the eschatological context, that of the fulfilment of history.[2] A further indication of Jesus' view of his death and resurrection in baptismal language comes at the transfiguration where, in conversation with Moses and Elijah, 'They spoke about his departure [exodus] which he was about to bring to fulfilment at Jerusalem' (Luke 9.31). Later Paul is to relate stories from the exodus to Christian baptism (1 Cor. 10.1–5). He also picks up the relationship between baptism and Jesus' death and resurrection (Rom. 6.1–4). Both of these approaches are incipient in the teaching of Jesus.

Jesus sees his mission as coming to fulfilment in the events in Jerusalem. His baptism in water leads to a baptism in blood. His mission as the Son proclaiming the kingdom of God comes to fulfilment in the servant suffering for his people, and bringing their redemption. This final act is the fulfilment of the mission which will lead ultimately to the transformation of the whole world when he returns again.

It is the risen Christ who commissions the disciples before his ascension to make disciples of all nations, baptizing 'in the name of the Father, and of the Son and of the Holy Spirit' (Matt. 28.19). It is consistent with what we have already seen of the way that the mission of Jesus quickly incorporates his disciples in mission, yet although it is too early to see this as a baptismal formula, as there was a variety of practice in the New Testament, the commission itself shows an integral relationship between making disciples and baptism.[3] The fruit of disciple-making is baptisms, and baptisms are a call to further disciple-making.

The Church and mission in Acts

The Pentecost event is another eschatological sign. The promised pouring out of the Spirit has now happened and is a sign of the coming 'great and glorious day of the Lord' (Acts 2.20). Jesus has been exalted to the right hand of God. As the Father had given him the Holy Spirit, Jesus now pours out the Holy Spirit upon his followers. Once again the revelatory event draws us into the mystery of the triune God. It also draws us into the mission of that God. Convicted by Peter's powerful Pentecost sermon the people ask what they should do in response.

> 'Repent and be baptized, every one of you, in the name of Jesus Christ so that your sins may be forgiven. And you will receive the gift of the Holy Spirit. The promise is for you and your children and for all who are far off – for all the Lord our God will call.' (Acts 2.38–39)

Thus baptism is a part of the mission as Peter conceives it. The breaking in of the future is in the coming of the Holy Spirit. It implies a mission to the Jews, 'you and your children', and implies a mission to the Gentiles 'all who are far off' (Eph. 2.13). These were to be things that the Church was to struggle with throughout the narrative of the book of Acts.

These words of Peter would later influence the main elements of baptismal liturgy, which include a sign of repentance, baptism in water, the use of the name of Jesus, and the outpouring of the Spirit. In Acts what we might call conversion and baptism are often close together, whereas for us they may be further apart.

Today the normal wording at baptism is '*N*, I baptize you in the name of the Father, and of the Son, and of the Holy Spirit. Amen.' A number of times in Acts we see baptism in the name of Jesus alone (2.38; 8.16; 10.48). Some Pentecostal churches have made a big issue of this and have reverted to 'Jesus only' baptism. Some theologians have questioned the Matthian baptizing 'in the name of the Father, and of the Son and of the Holy Spirit' as being authentic to Jesus as a Trinitarian formula. The problem is looking for a formulaic wording in the Scriptures that should be directly applied now. Considerable development would later take place within the Church over baptismal formulas.[4] We will see that baptism in the third century did not use any of these formulas and the Orthodox churches have developed their formula in the passive tense: '*N* is baptized . . .' Perhaps the controversies we see over Jesus'-name baptism or Trinitarian baptism come from our reading into the texts of Scripture something we wish to justify in our own practice, or use to make us distinct. While the Church may later have defined an essential wording, in Acts there is a sense of flux.

The words of Peter have also been fought over in battles to do with baptismal theology. 'Repent and be baptized' makes a neat slogan for those who would advocate only the baptism of adults. The implication taken is that repentance must precede baptism not just as a norm but as an absolute necessity, and it must be conscious and wholehearted. However, Peter mentions that 'the promise is for you and for your children'. Does this mean that on the day of Pentecost some children were baptized? The exact meaning and relation of children to baptism has been one of great discussion.[5] An important factor in this discussion are the household baptisms of the Philippian jailer in Acts 16.31–33 and of Stephanas in 1 Corinthians 1.16, for example. George Beasley-Murray sees six relevant references to household and baptism in the New Testament.[6] Considerable arguments have been fought over the rightness of infant baptism as justified by Scripture. Suffice it to say that in a missional situation where the mission is to people previously untouched by the gospel there is likely to be considerable conversion growth, with the effective norm being the baptism of adults. As the ancient world became Christianized, and particularly within the Roman Empire from the fourth century onwards, so the change began from most baptism candidates being adults to most being children as Christian parents wanted the promise of the gospel to be fully applied to their children. This was a switch from conversion growth to biological growth of the Church.

There are a number of accounts of baptisms in the book of Acts. However, if you look carefully at each story, there is no neat ordering of repentance, baptism and the operation of the Holy Spirit. At Pentecost, response to the message leads to repentance and baptism with the promise of sharing in the Pentecostal outpouring, but it is not mentioned how or in what order (Acts 2.37–41). In Samaria repentance and baptism comes first, and the Spirit comes later (Acts 8.1–17). In the case of Cornelius the Spirit came first and was the grounds on which the people were baptized (Acts 10). It is a mistake to try to get from Acts a neat ordering of pastoral practice. Indeed it might be seen that Acts has a number of rather messy narratives, including some baptized people whose Christian life is not what we would expect, as in Ananias and Sapphira (Acts 5.1–11) or Simon (Acts 8.9–25) or the Corinthian church (See 1 Corinthians, but especially chapter 1). In one way this is encouraging: if we struggle with getting our mission and baptism correct, we can take heart that the earliest Christians appear to have had the same problems.

The desire to find a normative order for pastoral practice, and a theological rationale also arises in the events of Acts 8. Here Philip, one of the original deacons has gone and evangelized in Samaria. His mission of proclaiming Christ, healing and deliverance, led to many believing and being baptized. However, the story explains that they did not receive the Holy Spirit, and thus the apostles come from Jerusalem to give the Holy Spirit by the laying on of hands. This was used for a long period to justify the practice of confirmation subsequent to baptism.[7] However, it is another example of trying to find a normative sequence to justify an existing practice. If 'repent and be baptized' is used to justify adult only baptism, then this has been used to justify confirmation. The most obvious way in which that happens is for the confirmation service to include this passage from Acts as a reading (although usually omitting the verses concerning miraculous healings and deliverance). It would seem more likely that these strange events occur because of the missiological flow of the book of Acts; Acts 1.8 talks about witnessing in Jerusalem, Judea, Samaria and the ends of the earth. Acts 8 is one of the key points at which mission is going further and further away from the Jewish centre into new fields that are ripe for harvest.[8] The book finishes at the end of the earth with Paul in Rome. Thus it is more likely that the events of Acts 8 occur because of a missiological turning point than that they were included for the justification of confirmation, which as we will see only really existed as an independent rite centuries later.

Some baptismal themes in the New Testament

While not wanting to look at every potential passage in the New Testament and the history of its interpretation, some themes have been particularly important (and sometimes fought over). They also have been influential on liturgies and thinking in terms of mission.

One such key passage comes from the discussion of Jesus and Nicodemus. 'Unless one is born of water and spirit you cannot enter the kingdom of God' (John 3.5). This is reiterated later with the phrase 'born of the Spirit' (John 3.8). The new age is the age of the Spirit and it was inaugurated in the coming of Jesus. The pouring out of the Spirit on Jesus at his baptism and on the Church at Pentecost all herald the age of the Spirit. Some commentators believe John has an incipient sacramentalism within his Gospel and interpret this passage as having a reference to baptism.[9] Baptism ushers people into the age of the Spirit. John 3 also raises questions of regeneration and baptism. Being born again is being regenerated, which in the Scriptures comes close together with baptism while for us there is often the pastoral issue of conversion and baptism being far apart. We will explore some of these themes later.

Another pole of baptismal theology is that of death and resurrection; this is particularly reflected in Romans.[10] 'All of us who were baptized into Christ Jesus were baptized into his death. We were therefore buried with him through baptism into death in order that, just as Christ was raised . . . we too might live a new life' (6.3–4).

We have already seen that Jesus saw his crucifixion and resurrection as a baptism, and one that his disciples would undertake. While this may point to the martyrdom of the apostles, it was also seen as more generally applicable here by Paul, who links our baptism to the death and resurrection of Christ and to our way of life. If a part of the baptismal calling is to be holy then this cannot be separated from witness. Why does Paul exhort his readers to a godly lifestyle? It is a part of calling people from among the Gentiles to the obedience of faith.

'One Lord, one faith, one baptism' (Eph. 4.5), connects baptism to unity, a significant theme in the time of the apostles and still the case today.[11] The God and Father of all is over all and in all. Our baptism brings us into the one Church, the agent of God in mission throughout the world. This is not to say that God cannot work outside the Church, but that the Church has a particular role in God's mission. Here Paul sees the danger of the lack of unity of the Spirit within the Church. If there is one body then there cannot be division, if there is one baptism then through that baptism we are one Church.[12] Striving for unity is to be faithful to the mission of God. Paul found he had to strive for unity a number of times, in the whole question of the validity and nature of Gentile mission, and in the relationships within churches and their witness to the surrounding society.

Many think that 1 Peter incorporates baptismal catechesis.[13] Baptism is mentioned using the type of Noah and the ark (1 Peter 3.20–21). Others have suggested that 'now that you have purified yourselves' (1.22) is the post-baptismal hinge of the book, which sets itself in the context of an early baptismal liturgy. This is an old theory, and is intriguing, but ultimately cannot be proved. However, we can see that the book is concerned that newborn babies are given spiritual milk and grow in the Lord; certainly a process of catechetical development. Perhaps most striking is the statement 'you are a chosen people, a royal priesthood, a holy nation' (2.9). This picks up themes from the Old Testament applying the language used for Israel to the Church. Peter had been chosen by Jesus and was sent as an apostle to proclaim the gospel. The people he is writing to have also been chosen and in that sense are also sent. As a royal priesthood they have a task to be intermediaries between God and the world. This takes its place in the preaching of the gospel, in intercession for the world and in a life of service. Priesthood and mission are not often considered as belonging together, and baptism as an inauguration into a royal priesthood gives weight to the gravity and privilege of the position and task given to us.

Rudimentary baptismal liturgy?

Are there elements from Acts which we may define as essential for any baptism? It would appear that water applied 'in the name . . .' is one aspect of early Church practice.[14] From the time of Pentecost, repentance would seem to be an aspect of baptism. Whether this was verbally articulated is open to question. It was probable that the actual baptism itself was seen as an act of repentance. A further element was perhaps some sort of profession of faith. The profession by the Ethiopian eunuch, 'I believe that Jesus Christ is the Son of God' in Acts 8.36, is not found in all ancient manuscripts but may indicate the practice of some apostolic churches. The confession 'Jesus is Lord' in 1 Corinthians, may also be rooted in a baptismal profession. Clearly there is a trajectory in the narrative of the New Testament that leads to a pattern of verbal repentance, confession of faith, and baptism 'in the name . . .' becoming part of an essential baptismal liturgy. These are rooted in the New Testament, but it will take some considerable time to frame all baptismal rites.

There are other elements within the New Testament that would later be included within baptismal liturgies, including *Common Worship*, but which may have been metaphorical rather than ritual. One is the metaphor of clothing, 'you who were baptized into Christ have been clothed with Christ' (Gal. 3.27).[15] This also may be related to the wedding garment in the parables of Jesus, and the person who is invited to the marriage feast (Matt. 22.1–14). Certainly in later centuries when baptism entailed significant amounts of water, a white garment was used at the baptism itself. Here the biblical text may have added to the rite. The other metaphor of particular significance is that of anointing, 'you have an anointing from the holy one' (1 John 2.20, 27). Anointing is mentioned a number of times in the New Testament and was to become a significant, and for some an essential part of baptismal liturgy.[16] Whereas in English we have the words 'anointed one', 'anointing', and 'oil', in Greek Christ, chrismation and chrism derive from the same word that better reveals their connection. Some have argued that the anointings in the New Testament are liturgical rather than metaphorical but it is not clear that is necessarily so.

There are other elements in our contemporary baptismal liturgy for which justification may be found in the New Testament, but it is clear that this is not absolutely essential for the New Testament. One such element is the renunciation of the devil, and maybe even an exorcism, as will be found in later rites. While there is a ministry of deliverance within the evangelistic practice of the apostolic Church, there are no examples of this being a preliminary within a baptismal liturgy. This seems to have developed in a later but still very early period, and be related to a dualistic view of the world with us either under the devil or under Christ.[17]

The other ceremony which may express the missiological calling of the baptized is the giving of a lighted candle. Although in the *Common Worship* service the candle comes at the end of the rite to show being sent out as lights in the world, it is a medieval development within the liturgy and originally not necessarily missional. While one is baptized into Christ as the light of the world, lights were not used as a part of early baptism.

Baptism in the *Didache*

The *Didache* is a much debated document, but may have been written at the same time as the Gospels and gives insight into the ordering of the Church, probably in the region of Syria.[18]

It begins with the statement, 'There are two ways, one to life and one to death', a common moral approach in the ancient world which in the *Didache* has been Christianized. Is this an evangelistic sermon or is it teaching in preparation for baptism? Certainly there are elements in this section which will later be put into catechetical preparation, once a catechumenate has developed within the Church. The two ways (chapters 1–7) comes immediately before the section on baptism and thus seems to be placed as pre-baptismal teaching. Preaching evangelistically and baptismal preparation merge into one event in baptism, like that of the Ethiopian.

Instructions on baptism in *Didache* 8 introduce two elements that are unusual for us. One is worrying about the quality of water used, and a preference for running water above water from cisterns (it would seem that water in cisterns could get warm). The other element is the importance of fasting. The candidate, the officiant, and others attending are all expected to fast for one or two days before the event itself. While there are still fast days within the calendar today, perhaps only now observed in part during Lent, there was a greater emphasis on fasting in the early Church as a spiritual discipline. To us this seems unusual as we tend not to practice fasting much or rate it highly, to them we might seem incredibly lax and lacking in spiritual character.

Twice the *Didache* mentions baptism 'in the name of the Father and of the Son and of the Holy Spirit'. Here we can see a strong connection with the Matthean Church, as seen in Matthew 28, and use of the triune name in a more formulaic role.

There is a further reference to baptism in *Didache* 9.5: 'Let no one eat or drink of your thanksgiving [meal] save those who have been baptized . . . Since the Lord has said concerning this "do not give what is holy to the dogs".' Here we come for the first time to a clear indication that baptism is necessary before receiving communion. At first sight it appears that the *Didache* is quoting from Matthew 7.27, but many people think that they are both drawing on a common oral tradition, particularly if the *Didache* is seen as written earlier than the Gospel.

What we do not find in the *Didache* is any direction about anointing, or clothing. Like Acts there is a fairly simple baptismal procedure, but it has developed its own agenda in questions about the water and fasting. It does show however that our now-familiar baptismal formula may have been in use from at least the time of the apostles in certain churches. By putting baptism in the context of the two ways, the *Didache* sets baptism within mission. It will, however, take some time, and a change in the context of the Church, before established baptismal liturgies become a part of its life.

Postscript

The Bible passages are of key significance not only as a historical record but also in the way they continue to shape the baptismal liturgy, and our theology of baptism. One important question they raise is for contemporary preaching, where outside a baptism there appears to be little teaching on the subject.

Common Worship provides lectionary material that could be used outside a baptismal service to preach on baptism. Bible readings and psalms are provided in supplementary texts which could be used for a short series of sermons.[19] The seasonal provision also has its own lectionary, which would be possible to use at the relevant time to teach on baptism and confirmation. The rubrics say 'these texts may be used on any occasion to meet pastoral circumstances'; one such circumstance would be to provide some teaching for the congregation. Developing a baptismal spirituality in a local congregation will require that there be frequent baptismal teaching and preaching.

Notes

1 George Beasley-Murray, 1962, *Baptism in the New Testament*, London: Macmillan; Arland J. Hultgren, 1994, '*Baptism in the New Testament: Origins, Formulas, and Metaphors*', in *Word & World*, 14, no. 1, pp. 6–11; A.Y. Collins, 1995, 'The Origin of Christian Baptism', in M. E. Johnson, *Living Water, Sealing Spirit*, New York: Pueblo, pp. 35–57; Paul F. Bradshaw, 1996, *Early Christian Worship: A Basic Introduction to Ideas and Practice*, Collegeville: Liturgical Press; Everett Ferguson, 2009, *Baptism in the Early Church: History, Theology, and Liturgy in the First Five Centuries*, Grand Rapids: William B. Eerdmans.

2 For eschatology and baptism see, Geoffrey Wainwright, 1969, *Christian Initiation*, Richmond: John Knox Press.

3 W. D. Davies and D.C. Allison, 1997, *The Gospel According to St Matthew: A Critical and Exegetical Commentary Vol. 3*, Edinburgh: T&T Clark.

4 E. C. Whitaker, 1961, 'The History of the Baptismal Formula', in *Journal of Ecclesiastical History* 16: 1–12.

5 Joachim Jeremias, 1964, *Infant Baptism in the First Four Centuries*, London: SCM Press.

6 Beasley-Murray, *Baptism*, pp. 312–20.

7 Phillip Tovey, 2014, *Anglican Confirmation: 1662–1820*, Farnham: Ashgate.

8 Vanmelitharayil John Samkutty, 2006, *The Samaritan Mission in Acts*, Edinburgh: T&T Clark.

9 R. E. Brown, 1966, *The Gospel According to John*, London: Geoffrey Chapman; W. Temple, 1947, *Readings in John's Gospel*, London: Macmillan.

10 M. Olusina Fape, 1999, *Paul's Concept of Baptism and Its Present Implications for Believers: Walking in the Newness of Life*, Lewiston: E. Mellen Press.

11 World Council of Churches, 2011, *One Baptism: Towards Mutual Recognition*, Faith and Order Paper 210, Geneva: World Council of Churches.

12 World Council of Churches, 1982, *Baptism, Eucharist and Ministry*, Faith and Order Paper 111, Geneva: World Council of Churches.

13 Ernest Best, 1971, *1 Peter*, New Century Bible, London: Oliphants.

14 Oscar Cullmann, 1950, *Baptism in the New Testament*, London: SCM, pp. 71–80.

15 Martin F. Connell, 2011, 'Clothing the body of Christ: An inquiry about the letters of Paul', in *Worship* 85, 2, pp. 128–46.

16 George D. Dragas, 2011, 'The seal of the gift of the Holy Spirit: the sacrament of chrismation', in *Greek Orthodox Theological Review* 56, 1–4, pp. 143–59.

17 Henry Ansgar Kelly, 1985, *The Devil at Baptism: Ritual, Theology, and Drama*, Ithaca: Cornell University Press.

18 Kurt Niederwimmer, 1998, *The Didache: A Commentary*, Minneapolis: Fortress Press.

19 Church of England, 2006, *Common Worship: Christian Initiation*, London: Church House Publishing, pp. 151, 157, 162, 167.

2

The Catechumenate as a Model for Mission

In post-apostolic times the treatise on the *Apostolic Tradition* of Hippolytus is an important document in the consideration of baptism and mission. We can see from Tertullian that there was a growing, complex baptismal rite, primarily for adults, which included anointing and hand-laying. Thus the primary symbol of water was attracting a set of secondary symbols around it, ones that develop various aspects of the primary symbol. Hippolytus seems to have given the first outline of a rite, and because of its antiquity was very important in the first round of twentieth-century liturgical revision, particularly in discussion of the catechumenate. It was believed that Hippolytus was early third century and gave us accurate information from an early period. However, further reflection has produced a more nuanced approach; the standard works on Hippolytus (Dix, 1937; Botte, 1946 and Cuming, 1976)[1] are reconstructions of a supposed original text. The manuscripts that exist today are partial documents in a number of languages. Later work (Bradshaw, 2002)[2] has caused us to be more cautious about what is said. This is in part because the key section on newcomers to the faith, the instruction for catechumens and those who are preparing for baptism are missing from the Latin text (quite possibly pages have been lost) and thus to make categorical statements about what is happening in Rome at this time is going beyond the evidence. However, having added that caution, it is reasonable to follow the document, particularly where it is ratified in other writings of the same era.

Even before the ending of the persecution of the Church, her mission was strong and people came to faith. As the Church grew in numbers so it would seem that churches developed catechetical systems of dealing with new people. A catechumen is someone who is under instruction in preparation for their baptism. We still use the root of the word in 'catechism', which is a teaching document in preparation for further initiation. Thus classically within Anglicanism the catechism is used before confirmation, and there may be some people around today who learned it off by heart, either older people in this country or people in other parts of the Anglican Communion. In the early Church the catechumenate developed to prepare people for baptism and was a period of preparation of various lengths. Not only was there a listening to the word, but there are also various catechetical rites in which the candidate participated.

In the Roman Empire the state was to have a change of heart about the Church. At first it was suspicious and Christians were persecuted. This led to the cult of martyrs, and the view that those who had witnessed to their faith by death, but who had missed baptism itself, were baptized in their own blood. Persecution also brought problems with what to do with the reincorporation of those who lapsed during persecution; once persecution ceased many wanted to rejoin the Church. How were they recognized as fully included in baptismal grace once more? Hippolytus perhaps indicated a further phase when society was more open to the Church, many were coming in and the Church wanted to give greater regulation to those who asked for baptism. If the situation had been of 'culture against Christ', now the situation was becoming 'Church cautiously welcoming the culture' and having an increased impact on it.

The catechetical process in Hippolytus

The process begins with those coming forward to hear the word for the first time. At this point various questions are asked of them, although it would appear to be in a more informal way; questions about whether they are a slave or free, married or not, possessed or not. Various professions were forbidden for those who wished to be baptized at this time; this is in line with discussions in other documents. It is possible to classify the professions that are rejected in three areas; the sex industry, idolatry and magic, and professions that may involve the persecution of Christians. These areas of work seemed to be strictly prohibited, although work as a magistrate and in the army begin to become more acceptable as the nation becomes Christian. So provided you are not in a prohibited employment, have a master who is willing for you to hear, and a husband who is willing for you to listen, you can be enrolled as a catechumen.

Hippolytus then continues to say that the catechumen should hear the word for three years. This gives the impression of a highly extended catechumenate, but it would appear that this did not happen in a simple programmatic way and the length of the catechumenate was not this long in other places. We shall see how it actually worked when we later come to look at the experience of Augustine. There seems to be only a simple ritual blessing associated at this point. The catechumen continues to hear the word; presumably this means either the first half of the Eucharist, the ministry of the word, or in a separate catechumenal lecture. The catechumens leave before the peace and are not allowed to participate in it 'for their peace is not yet holy'. The end of the catechumenal session includes the laying on of hands by the teacher (whether ordained or lay). However, Hippolytus then goes on to discuss the martyrdom of catechumens and the baptism in blood, which suggests that in some way the catechumen is in the Church rather than outside it. The catechumenate caused reconsideration of the boundaries of the Church, and expectations at different levels.

A new phase, one more intensive, happens when the catechumen is chosen to be baptized. The beginning of the second phase of the catechumenate starts with what some call a scrutiny. At this point a number of questions are asked about them and their Christian lifestyle. They even change their status within the prayers, no longer catechumens but elect.

From the scrutiny onwards there is an intensive period of hand laying and exorcising. The period varies in length between churches, but it would seem to be the origins of the Sundays in Lent, where various later works give readings and indications of teaching and liturgy going together in this preparation period.[3] In the ancient world superstition, idolatry and magic were quite common. Thus a dualistic cosmology of the kingdom of darkness and the kingdom of light may well sit behind this exorcist activity, although the people of the time would properly want to distinguish between those actually possessed and those whose bad lifestyle indicated what we might call their inner demons.[4] Later theology made a distinction between major and minor exorcisms, the baptismal rite being a minor exorcism.

This more intensive period involved the bishop, who himself was involved in laying on of hands and exorcising. This was preparatory for the catechumens coming to the vigil in which they would receive baptism, Eucharist, and be incorporated into the Church. It would appear that this happened at Easter, and is the origin of our Easter vigil, but that does not exclude it happening in other parts of the Christian Church at other times of the year, for example Epiphany and Pentecost.

The baptism begins with a night of vigil where the candidates continue receiving intensive instruction. At first light the font is prepared with the water. People are baptized naked, even removing any ornaments they have. In some parts of the world this led to the importance of the deaconess who would be involved in anointing the women. Instructions are given for those who cannot speak for themselves (for example, children) although clearly the rite is primarily for the adults. Preparations are then made of various oils; indeed we will see that a feature of the rite is the use of at least three different sorts of oil. There is also a large cast of clergy within the service; deacons, priests and a bishop are all required. The service begins with a renunciation of Satan and anointing with the oil of exorcisms. The candidate is then handed over to the bishop or priest for baptism.

It is in the middle of the description of the baptism that the Latin text resumes. At this point the candidate is standing in the water possibly with a deacon next to them while they are being quizzed, possibly by a priest, about their faith. In Hippolytus it happens in this way: first the candidate is asked if they believe in God the Father, and on saying they believe they are immersed; then they are asked if they believe in Jesus Christ, and on saying they believe, they are immersed; finally they are asked if they believe in the Holy Spirit and on saying they believe again they are immersed. There is clearly some link between this baptismal practice and the Apostles Creed. Today we might ask questions and do one immersion; in the time of Hippolytus it would appear that there were immersions after each question. At the end of this section a presbyter anoints them with oil in the name of Jesus and they enter into the church.

As in any liturgical activity, the actual nature of the building is quite significant. There are many examples in the early Church of churches where the baptistery is in a separate building. This can be clearly seen in St John Lateran in Rome, in the baptistery in Florence, and in Kurian on Cyprus, the church being built at the time of the Council of Nicaea. Where this is so, many of the rites described so far may be occurring in the baptistery and may be somewhat separate from the gathered congregation who are in the neighbouring basilica.

On their entry into the church the bishop lays hands on them thanking God that they have received remission of sins and regeneration of the Holy Spirit and asks for further grace. He anoints them again, and signs them again with the sign of the cross. After the peace from the bishop they are then able for the first time to give the kiss of peace to the whole congregation.

The service then continues with the Eucharist in a normal sort of way, save that there is an extra cup of milk and honey indicating entering into the promised land.

Catechumenate and mission

This extended description of what happens in Hippolytus is important as it gives us a very different picture from what was happening earlier, although in both cases we are working with sparse evidence. It is also important to look at this, as it is unlike what we do, not least in restricting the peace to Church members. This book is a journey through sections of history which, by their very nature, will be different from us today.

The catechumenate appears at one level to fit the 'attractive' system of organizing many people into coming into Church. Its length gives the possibility of a proper preparation, although the three years given by Hippolytus are not universally held as some sort of norm. While part of the teaching would seem to be general biblical teaching, there is a clear concern about this working through into Christian ethical behaviour. The scrutiny at the beginning of the intensive phase asked questions such as, have you visited widows or the sick? This is, perhaps, in contrast to our catechism which is primarily doctrinal, or to more modern courses, such as Alpha which include experience of the Spirit. Indeed we know that there was a certain amount of reticence in giving some basic texts to people undergoing the process, including texts such as the Lord's Prayer. This must have made some of what occurred during the initiation process quite baffling to the candidates, and there are series of sermons of an explicative nature explaining all of the symbolic actions to them, but after (not before) the event has occurred.[5]

It may be that the mission of the Church is partially being shaped by the society in which it exists. As the Church comes more into the centre of public life and it begins to have large buildings in which it can operate, so the more informal house church style of worship needs to change. There have been some suggestions of an unconscious inculturation of aspects of mystery religion or at least of a more phased initiation, and thus a complicated process resulted in these more complex liturgies (one is tempted to say 'anything you can do, I can do better'; the Church outdoing the mystery religions). It is certainly true that mystery religions and Christianity could share space quite close together, as can be seen in San Clemente in Rome where a Mythratic temple is right next to a place of Christian worship.

Apparently one of the things the Church was trying to achieve through the catechumenate was to continue to hold high the bar of Christian standards. The martyrs had died for their faith, and with the end of the era of martyrdom comes a relaxing of the demands of the Christian life. The catechumenate could at least help those from outside the Church gain some knowledge of Christian truth and feel the demands of Christian ethics. It must be remembered, however, that the relaxing of persecution in the Roman Empire, as it became Christian, was bad news for Christians in the Persian Empire, where they now could possibly be seen as spies and traitors.

The case of Augustine

Of interest in this discussion is the example of Augustine. While he is later than Hippolytus and has links with Milan rather than Rome we can see that the tidy-minded pastoral approach of a Church order does not actually work out with real people.

Augustine was born in 354 in modern-day Algeria and was a Berber, although from a very Romanized family. So we are looking at the operation of the catechumenate over 100 years later than Hippolytus. Augustine's mother was a Christian when he was born, but his father was not, and he notes that 'even from the womb of my mother' he was marked with the cross salted with salt.[6] This is certainly a reference to the rite for making a catechumen and seems to imply that it happened before he was able to answer for himself. The system that was once used primarily for adults is now being extended to infants. When he was sick as a child his family considered having him baptized, but when he recovered this was stopped from the fear of post-baptismal sin, which was regarded as worse than sin before baptism. This type of belief led many people to be made a catechumen, only to be baptized on their deathbed. Emperor Constantine was to follow this pattern.

While technically a member of the Christian Church, Augustine strayed considerably. He went to study rhetoric in Carthage and settled down with a mistress, with whom he had a son, and took up an interest in Manicheism, a sect. So he had both in practice and in thought abandoned the Christian faith. In 382 he went to Italy which changed his life profoundly, not least in meeting Ambrose who was Bishop of Milan. Augustine therefore determined to become a catechumen again; it is not clear whether there was any ritual for this but it certainly involved listening to the sermons of Ambrose. He gave up his teaching role and in his villa studied the Psalms with a friend, who was also a catechumen. Augustine's catechumenate included his own personal study, but then he was a significant professor of the day. He was baptized on Easter Day 387 with his son, and his long-time friend. His final catechumenate had lasted less than a year and he records his great joy both at being baptized and in the ceremony of the service. He was to go on to be one of the most influential figures in Western theology of baptism.

His life illustrates the problems of the catechumenate. What do you do when as a mother you are the only Christian in the family? Monica is perhaps a long-suffering example of perseverance in this area. But we can also see that the Church is forced to respond to the anxieties of parents, in a number of ways. The first is the inclusion of children in the rituals, in this case making Augustine a catechumen. Second, there are the anxieties of post-baptismal sin: this was a significant issue for many people at this time, and ironically it is Augustine's theology that will end this. Third, we see how a catechumen can stray considerably from the Christian way. Augustine seems to be driven by a deep sense of his sin in this area. Finally, we see a short catechumenate before baptism which seems to involve listening to sermons, which may have been an earlier part of the process, and a considerable amount of personal study. Augustine was certainly not going to do it in any standard way. We can see that he was very moved by the baptismal ceremonies, and impressed by the character of Ambrose. However one might want to make any system a neat package there will always be people who do not fit. Here is a good early Church example.

Mystagogy and song

Teaching did not finish after baptism but continued for some time afterwards. This post-baptismal period is called a period of mystagogy. We are fortunate that this part of the process has been preserved, and that mystagogical sermons from some of the great preachers of the time were written down. Thus we have the sermons of Ambrose, Cyril of Jerusalem, John Chrysostom, and Theodore of Mopsuestia.[7]

These sermons go through the initiation process explaining their meaning in the light of the Scriptures and the salvation of the candidate. Thus Cyril of Jerusalem says of the baptism:

> You made the confession that brings salvation, and submerged yourselves three times in the water and emerged: by this symbolic gesture you were secretly re-enacting the burial of Christ three days in the tomb.[8]

He explains anointing after baptism in a similar fashion:

> Christ was anointed with the spiritual oil of gladness because he is the author of spiritual joy; and you have been anointed with chrism because you have become fellows and sharers of Christ.[9]

Thus we have a rich explanation of the different baptismal rites from different places. There is clearly some variation both of actual detail of the rites and of the method of explanation of what had happened to the candidates. However, these sermons from a later period of the catechumenate give us a deeper understanding of the theological and liturgical approach of the church at the time.[10]

Also of interest are a series of hymns of the Epiphany by the great hymn writer Ephraim the Syrian. It is not clear how these hymns were used, but there may be a liturgical use in the services of baptism at Epiphany, the Eastern Church seeing Epiphany rather than Easter as one of the key baptismal times of the year. It is also possible that the hymns had a catechetical role, people studying some of them as a way of learning the Christian faith.[11]

Ephraim connects the baptism of Jesus and the baptism of the candidates:

The Spirit came down from on high,
and hallowed the waters by his brooding.
In the baptism of John,
He passed by the rest and abode on One:
but now he has descended and abode,
on all that are born of the water.[12]

Here is a rich and complex mixture of allusions to Genesis, the baptism of Jesus and the baptism of a candidate (see Gen. 1.2, Matt. 3.16). It is the Spirit who descends on those who are baptized in the water. This is the first of 20 verses with a refrain:

Blessed be He who was baptized that He might baptize you,
that you should be absolved from your offences.[13]

Jesus' baptism and our baptism are intimately connected.

The hymns for the feast of Epiphany are a series of 15 hymns. In three there is a meditation on chrism:

Christ and chrism are conjoined;
the secret with the visible is mingled:
the chrism anoints visibly, Christ seals secretly,
the lambs new-born and spiritual,
the prize of his twofold victory;
for He engendered it of the chrism,
and He gave it birth of the water.[14]

Here we can see some of the development of the theology of anointing. The hymn goes on to meditate about the place of oil within the Scriptures and how Old Testament stories prefigure the coming of Christ. The refrain makes clear the purpose of anointing: Christ is sealing the newborn lambs in his flock.

Thus there were rich resources in preaching and song which were used in the baptismal rite and the catechumenal process. These sermons and hymns alongside the Church orders give us clarity about the catechumenate as the mission strategy for the early Church.

Catechumenate in Anglican mission

In Chapter 3 we will see what happens to the catechumenate and baptism in the medieval period, but I want to discuss now the development of missionary societies within Anglicanism which began with the Society for the Propagation of the Gospel (SPG) and the Society for Promoting Christian Knowledge (SPCK) at the beginning of the eighteenth century, and which developed with the Church Missionary Society (CMS) and others in the nineteenth century. Thomas Bray was influential in starting the first two missionary societies and developed a significant system of catechizing around preparation for confirmation. In adapting this to the Americas it had to be preparation for admission to communion because of a lack of bishops for confirmation; no bishops went to America before independence. Later on, more developed catechumenates were used by Anglican missionaries and we can see in the peak of empire the development of rites of admission of catechumens in India, Japan and Africa.[15] This is a story perhaps undeveloped, but it certainly seems to have occurred with a look back at the story above. Anglicanism was confronted by either people from a completely different religious background, or from a primal religion background. This was work in a totally different context from Europe and other parts of the world where some Christian knowledge can be assumed. The idea that there could be a number of years of teaching prior to baptism for adults was thus one that was attractive and operated by the missionaries.

A different type of development of the catechumenate occurred after the Second Vatican Council. The Roman Catholic Church revised its rites of adult initiation with the *Rite of Christian Initiation of Adults* produced in 1972.[16] People were aware in many westernized societies of a drift away from Christian faith, and of significant numbers of adults who had scant knowledge of Christian faith. So a fuller preparation process including a mixture of rituals and teaching was an attractive package.

This approach has been adopted in a number of Anglican Provinces including the Episcopal Church, the Anglican Church of Canada, and the Church in Wales.[17] It has also been adopted by some Lutherans.[18] Thus there has been a wide movement in a renewed catechumenate.

In the Church of England this was first promulgated by a small group of enthusiasts particularly around the writings of Peter Ball.[19] This was then picked up in the report *On the Way* which looked for a more holistic approach to evangelism than simple conversion, and an approach to baptism that was more than a family affair in the afternoon.[20] The aim is that a parish would be a baptising community, rather than a Christian community in which the vicar did everything to do with baptism.[21] The report also looked at the place of schools and ethical teaching in preparation for baptism or confirmation. As such it has a wider mission and vision than simply fishing for individuals.

This was finally developed into the services in *Common Worship: Christian Initiation*, in the section 'Rites on the Way: Approaching Baptism'.[22] Here are a set of pastoral rites that have tried to avoid the archaic language of the catechumenate, but do catechumenal-type things in the sense that it anticipates a group of people learning together and being introduced to, and prayed for by, a congregation which will be involved at every step of their preparation. There have been some churches that have enthusiastically taken on such an approach, and have reported significant success in Christian formation. It has to be said also that either because of inertia or ignorance this section of *Common Worship* may be, for some parishes, a completely unknown area.

It is still true in some places that baptism is seen as the minister's job. This means that church members are not involved in the process, and then when people turn up in large numbers for baptism the congregation is resentful of their presence. If the church becomes a baptizing community then all have a role in baptismal preparation, in prayer, hospitality, teaching, mentoring. If the church is conceived of by way of baptismal ecclesiology then it makes more sense for catechumenal rites to exist and for them to become significant in a local congregation. At root here there are questions of ecclesiology as much as pastoral practice, and a failure of the every member ministry approach of previous generations to have pushed through into significant change in the baptismal ministry of the Church.

Postscript

The catechumenate is thus an evolving model that connects mission and baptism. It is used both in the ancient and modern world as a way of Christian formation of disciples in preparation for baptism. It challenges the clericalization of the Church and can open baptism into the life of the whole Christian community. The catechumenate died out with the development of infant baptism. The catechumenate has to be seen in the context of adult baptism being the normative way of entry into the church and the fruit of mission.

Notes

1 G. Dix, 1937, *Apostolic Paradosis: The Treatise on the Apostolic Tradition of St Hippolytus of Rome*, New York: Macmillan; B. Botte, 1946, *Hippolyte de Rome: La Tradition Apostolique*, Paris: Cerf; G. J. Cuming, 1976, *Hippolytus: A Text for Students*, GLS 8, Bramcote: Grove Books.

2 Paul F. Bradshaw, Maxwell E. Johnson, Edward L. Phillips, 2002, *The Apostolic Tradition: A Commentary*, Minneapolis: Fortress Press.

3 Leonel L. Mitchell, 1991, *Worship: Initiation and the Churches*, Washington, DC: Pastoral Press, pp. 17–47.

4 See Colossians 1.13, and Henry Ansgar Kelly, 1985, *The Devil at Baptism: Ritual, Theology, and Drama*, Ithaca: Cornell University Press.

5 See Edward Yarnold, 1972, *The Awe-Inspiring Rites of Initiation: Baptismal Homilies of the Fourth Century*, Slough: St Paul Publications.

6 Augustine, 1991, *The Confessions of Saint Augustine*, Trans. E. B. Pusey, New York: Quality Paperback Book Club, p. 12.

7 Yarnold, *Rites of Initiation*.

8 Yarnold, *Rites of Initiation*, p. 76.

9 Yarnold, *Rites of Initiation*, p. 80.

10 Enrico Mazza, 1989, *Mystagogy: A Theology of Liturgy in the Patristic Age*, New York: Pueblo.

11 Philip Schaff and Henry Wace, 1983, *A Select Library of Nicene and Post-Nicene Fathers of the Christian Church, Second Series, Ephraim Syrus*, Vol. 8 Part 2, Grand Rapids: Eerdmans.

12 Schaff and Wace, *Select Library*, p. 273.

13 Schaff and Wace, *Select Library*, p. 273.

14 Schaff and Wace, *Select Library*, p. 269.

15 H. P. Thompson, 1933, *Worship in Other Lands*, London: SPG.

16 The Roman Catholic Church, 1976, 1983, *The Rites*, New York: Pueblo.

17 The Episcopal Church, 1988, *The Book of Occasional Services*, 2nd edn, New York: Church Hymnal Corporation; The Church in Wales, 2006, *Services for Christian Initiation*, Norwich: Canterbury Press; Anglican Church of Canada, *Making Disciples*, www.anglican.ca/faith/worship/catechumenate/ (accessed 2014).

18 Lutheran Church in America, 1997, *Occasional Services*, Minneapolis: Augsburg Publishing House.

19 Peter Ball, 1988, *Adult Believing: A Guide to the Christian Initiation of Adults*, New York: Paulist Press.

20 General Synod, 1995, *On the Way: Towards an Integrated Approach to Christian Initiation*, GS Misc 444, London: Church House Publishing.

21 A. Theodore Eastman, 1982, *The Baptizing Community: Christian Initiation and the Local Congregation*, New York: Seabury Press.

22 See Church of England, 2006, *Common Worship: Christian Initiation*, London: Church House Publishing, pp. 15–56.

3

The Middle Ages and Mission in a Christian Society

The Middle Ages is a long and complex period of history. The mission of the Church was carried out in many and various ways with the evangelization and sometimes re-evangelization of tribes in northern Europe, the increasing threat of Islam in the east, the expansion of the church to China and India by the Eastern Church and the need to feed and grow Christian people in Christian societies. In some places evangelization led to the conversion of adults and thus the baptism of adults. In other places that were Christianized the switch occurs primarily to infant baptism and generational growth. In some places whole tribes are converted in one go and baptized en masse leaving an ongoing problem of catechizing. The divisions of the Church, particularly in the east with non-Chalcedonian churches, led to transfer growth in mission. This chapter will look at some of the key issues in this period, particularly where they continue to affect the Church today.

Growth of infant baptism

The catechumenate, which was adopted across the whole Church was, as a mission strategy, primarily for adults, although including infants. In the whole process a person was introduced to Christianity, spiritually prepared, received teaching, baptized, received into the eucharistic community, and had follow up (mystagogy). Gradually in some places the candidates became primarily children, rather than adults. This was in part because of a success in mission, society that was once hostile had now embraced Christianity, and a Christian society is one of the key concepts of this period.

The early rites expected the baptismal candidates to answer for themselves, as they were adult. We have seen in Hippolytus and Augustine that this was the pattern. A change occurs and gradually we see in the text of the baptismal rite that the majority of candidates are expected to be infants. So in Rome at the time of John the Deacon, *c.* 500, we see in his letter that the candidates are still adults and children.[1] There is also the clear division between a first stage of making a catechumen, and then a second stage of the election before baptism. By the time of the Gelasian sacramentary (seventh century) the candidates are assumed to be children.[2] But the rite still assumes that the elements are divided up through the period of Lent leading to a climax of baptism at the Easter vigil and anointing with chrism by the bishop.

In these services people are expected to answer for their children through the various preparatory rites and within the baptismal rite itself. Thus the only substitution is for an adult to answer for the child, but the rites are still spread over a number of weeks in preparation for baptism. By the time of the Sarum rite (eleventh century) all the rites have been telescoped together into one service, thus the candidate admitted to the catechumenate, receives all the exorcisms, and is baptized all in one go.[3] This makes for a rather repetitive rite and one that is certainly very long. When things have been spaced out over a number of weeks they may appear to be edifying and illustrative of the gospel truth, when they are telescoped together the appearance is more of vain repetition. While the Church has adapted the liturgy for the new context in which the candidates are primarily infants, the liturgy itself is still basically a rite for adults in which infant candidates are answering by proxy. The rites up until the Reformation were such that all people who came for baptism were made a catechumen and then baptized. The system showed itself to be rather conservative!

But there were further changes to the system. Some regretted that the Church did not keep the more demanding approach of the early Church. However, underlying the developments there is a change in ecclesiology. If Church and culture are separate and antagonistic it is easy to hold a gathered Church ecclesiology with a high bar of entry. However, we should not over romanticize the early Church because as we have seen there may have been a high bar for baptism, but there seems to have been a fairly easy entry into the catechumenate and this was the point that people were deemed to be 'in' rather than 'out' of the Church. Questions of boundaries surround baptism by its very nature as the initiation sacrament. Augustine himself developed a more mixed Church model of ecclesiology resting on the parable of the wheat and tares, and this of course was a model that continued after the Reformation in established churches.

Augustine's theology of baptism was particularly significant in the West, not least the notion of original sin. The emphasis on the necessity of baptism and its requirement for saving grace, stopped people delaying baptism until near death. Indeed it pushed the need for infant baptism, rather than simply an infant catechumenate. This meant that delaying baptism, particularly with high infant mortality, was not an option. So how was the Church to respond to this problem? Baptism became increasingly performed not by the bishop at Easter in the cathedral, but by the presbyter in the parish church the Sunday after the birth. People could not delay the baptism of their children if their salvation were dependent upon it. The Augustinian theology of original sin has continued to influence the Western Church up to the present day. The *Catechism of the Catholic Church* says:

> Born with a fallen human nature and tainted by original sin, children also have need of the new birth in baptism to be free from the power of darkness and brought into the realm of freedom of the children of God.[4]

The Book of Common Prayer baptismal service has similar language:

> Forasmuch as all men are conceived and born in sin, and that our Saviour Christ saith, none can enter into the kingdom of

God, except he be regenerate and born anew of water and the Holy Ghost.[5]

This is bolstered by Article 9 which talks of 'this infection of nature' and the 'fault and corruption of every man [sic]'.[6] One step away from this was made in the rubrics on emergency baptism in the *Alternative Service Book* (1980) where it says that parents should be assured that questions of ultimate salvation do not depend on whether or not the child has been baptized (para. 106).[7] This was the first liturgical step away from the prevailing doctrine of original sin and its relationship to baptism in the Church of England.

There is a further consequence of the growth of infant baptism. In the model where adult baptism is the norm catechesis occurs prior to baptism and after baptism in mystagogical teaching. This can be seen ritualized in the delivery of key texts such as the Lord's Prayer or Creed, which were to be memorized by the catechumens, and also in sermons delivered in Lent for catechumens. Finally in the post-baptismal period we have splendid examples from Ambrose, John Chrysostom, Cyril of Jerusalem and Theodore of Mopsuestia where they explain in detail all the different elements of the rite that people have participated in, but may not have ever seen prior to their initiation. With the switch to infant baptism catechesis moves to after the baptismal event. Thus exhortations are included within the baptismal service that there should be memorization of elements such as the Lord's Prayer, the Apostles' Creed, and the Hail Mary by the candidate later in life. Rather than being a requirement for baptism these elements now become a requirement for confirmation. The changeover from conversion growth to biological growth also entails the changeover in the place of catechesis in Christian discipleship.

Integrated initiation with children

In some places there was a desire to fully initiate the candidate even as a child into the Christian life. Thus in the East the baptismal rites included elements of the catechumenate greatly truncated, baptism itself, chrismation, and reception of the Eucharist. This process can be seen in the Byzantine rite where, when baptism is conducted after a Liturgy,[8] eucharistic elements will be saved and administered to the child immediately after their baptism.

A slightly different pattern was practised in early Spain where all of the episcopal rites were delegated to the presbyter. Thus candidates were made catechumens, baptized, anointed and given Holy Communion. A letter from Eugene Bishop of Toledo to Braulio of Zaragoza, in the seventh century, asks questions about the administration of chrism by a deacon and the consecration of chrism by a presbyter. The answer seems to be that chrism cannot be consecrated by presbyter but may be administered by a deacon. However, within the correspondence it is clear that full initiation is conducted by the priest, and there is no need for a bishop to be present.[9] So there is no separate rite of confirmation, such prayers being conducted by the priest with the use of episcopally blessed oil. This approach can be seen liturgically in the *Liber Ordinum*, an eleventh-century book, where throughout the whole service, of 'an order of baptism for occasional use', the minister is the priest.[10] The service begins with catechumenal exorcisms, proceeds to the blessing of the font, and then after renunciation and profession baptizes the naked infant in the font. The infant is then clothed and anointed with chrism. The priest then places a hand on the child and asks for the perfection of the gift and prays for the gift of the sevenfold Spirit upon the child. The service continues with the rubric, 'the priest sets a veil over the head of the baptized infants, and communicates them'. The infant is thus fully initiated.

The Ambrosian Manual and the account of Beroldus give us an indication of what happened in Milan in the tenth and twelfth centuries.[11] The Manual has two orders of baptism. One has elements throughout Lent and culminates in an Easter baptism, the other is a stand-alone rite. In the first order on the second Sunday of Lent the names of candidates for baptism are given. There are then a series of scrutinies up to Palm Sunday. This includes the distinct exorcisms of ashes and the use of the goatskin. On the fifth Saturday the creed is delivered. In this rite there is also a renunciation of the devil. During the Easter vigil there is a complex blessing of the font including an adjuration of the water ('I adjure thee O creature of water' – a type of exorcism). There is then a question and answer version of the profession of faith, followed by baptism with a short litany of the saints being sung. After baptism the infants are anointed with chrism by a presbyter and the bishop washes the feet of the infants. Beroldus says that the archbishop does the anointing, but it is clear from the stand-alone rite that this may be done by the presbyter. It is also clear from that rite that the children are then given communion. Thus there would seem to be a pattern in Milan of baptism, chrismation and communion. If the bishop is present then the chrismation may be performed by the bishop, but otherwise it may be performed by a presbyter. The rite is performed around Easter, but can also be performed at other times of the year. The Lenten ceremonies are shorter than in some other places, perhaps a concession to the age of the candidates. Thus a connection is held between Easter and baptism. No particular element of the rite is reserved to the bishop, save that of the washing of feet. It is also clear that the candidates are all infants. So Milan was also able to hold onto a unified rite, partially by not asking for anything to be uniquely reserved to the bishop.

The Stowe Missal was written in Ireland about 800 and combines local rites and Roman elements.[12] It begins its order of baptism with a number of catechumenal ceremonies including the consecration of salt, pronunciations and professions of faith, and anointing of candidates. The blessing of the water begins with an exorcism and then a blessing in a particularly long prayer. Chrism is poured into the water. The candidate is then questioned by a deacon as to their belief, and baptized. They are anointed with chrism on the forehead and clothed in a white garment. The feet of the candidates are washed and the candidate receives communion. Once again the whole complex of Christian initiation occurs in one event, although this time it is not clear that it is connected to Easter. There is no reservation of any element to the bishop, and thus a deacon and presbyter can perform the whole rite.

Disintegration of initiation

In other places, particularly in Rome, the pattern was different. The elements of the previous unified rite that belonged to the bishop were reserved to the bishop only and baptism would have to be completed later in some way with an episcopal visit. Such an approach is found in the 25th epistle of Pope Innocent (402–417) to Decentius. Innocent answers a question about the anointing of those baptized by presbyters and gives a very forthright answer.

> It is permitted priests, when they baptize, either apart from the bishop or in his presence, to anoint the newly baptized with chrism [which would have been consecrated by the bishop] but it is not allowed to priests to anoint the forehead with the same holy oil, this being the exclusive prerogative of the Bishop in imparting the Holy Spirit.[13]

The time was one of turmoil with various invasions of Italy occurring. Clearly the question was asked because the practice was happening. However it does point to papal authority insisting on particular episcopal actions in Christian initiation. This was not much of a problem when dioceses were small and bishops could get around parishes so any element of delay might be quite short, but in northern Europe dioceses were quite large. One indication of this might be the medieval Diocese of Lincoln which stretched from the Humber to the Thames. There was no way the bishops would be able to complete the rites of initiation soon after baptism, but they did perform a separate service which has now become completely separated from baptism itself. This rite came to be called confirmation. It was not until the eighth century that this came to be discussed as a separate rite. Nonetheless, the influence of Rome led to its approach becoming the norm for most of the West.

The disintegration and separation into separate rites of a unified Christian initiation entails a number of divisions.[14] First, the separation of confirmation from baptism, second, removing the reception of communion from initiation, third, separating initiation from the festivals of Easter and or Pentecost, and fourth, fragmenting one rite into three parts, baptism, confirmation and reception of Holy Communion, increasingly separated by large intervals of time. When baptism was at the Easter vigil where adults and infants were baptized, anointed and received Holy Communion there was one combined service of initiation. This is now divided into a baptism in the parish church, followed by confirmation a number of years later, with a service of first communion which may be before or after confirmation. It is Peter Lombard who in the twelfth century first defines the seven sacraments, one of which is confirmation. Aquinas sees confirmation as a separate sacrament in which we are strengthened with an increase of grace. The Council of Florence defines the material of confirmation being chrism and the form being,

> I sign you with the sign of the cross and confirm you with the chrism of salvation, in the name of the Father, and of the Son, and of the Holy Spirit.

The minister is the bishop.

The liturgical books do not write separate services of confirmation as such, and we will see below that in the Sarum Manual confirmation is included later as a separate section. There is also considerable evidence of the neglect of confirmation by the laity. This led to the Council of Lambeth under Archbishop Peckham in 1281 requiring that people should be confirmed before they came to receive Holy Communion. This requirement continued after the Reformation with the rubric in the Book of Common Prayer requiring that 'none would be admitted to Holy Communion: until such time as he be confirmed' (1549). This was later modified to be confirmed or 'ready and desirous' to be confirmed (1662). In this there was continuity of practice.

If confirmation is to be separate from baptism, the question arises at what age one should be confirmed. The Prayer Book continues the medieval language of the 'years of discretion'. This is the medieval idea of when one comes to a point of responsibility for one's actions and thoughts, which was often regarded as about seven years old. The idea also had the unfortunate effect of reinforcing the detachment of baptism and confirmation. *Ordo Romanus* 11 (late sixth century) describes initiation in Rome.[15] After the preparation of the font, the children are baptized and chrismated by a presbyter. They are vested and stand before the Pope who says a prayer invoking the seven graces of the Holy Spirit. He then signs them with the cross in chrism. After this they go to the mass and the infants receive communion. Here we see a united service of baptism, 'confirmation', and the Eucharist. However in 1215 the Fourth Lateran Council stated that communion was not obligatory until the 'years of discretion', because baptized infants before that age could not lose the baptismal grace. Thus the concept of the age of discretion has led to a sundering of baptism on the one hand and confirmation and the Eucharist on the other. The logic of this type of trajectory leads to baptism as an infant, confirmation later in life, and first communion as a separate rite. This medieval pattern is still prevalent in Western churches.

Defining baptism

In the thirteenth century the rediscovery of Greek philosophy led to an Aristotelian movement in theology, in which Thomas Aquinas was particularly important. Part of this was the need to precisely define the sacraments. People needed to know if the sacrament was valid or not. A person who came to church having been baptized in some sort of sect that was deemed invalid would need to be validly baptized for the first time. Thus the Church wished to define what it called the 'form', the 'matter' and 'intention' of each sacrament.

The Council of Florence in 1439 said that there were three things necessary for a sacrament, the material, the form and the ministrant. All three need to be together for the sacraments to be accomplished. The material of baptism is the water. The form is 'I baptize you in the name of the Father, and of the Son, and of the Holy Spirit' or 'by my hand N is baptized in the name of the Father, and of the Son, and of the Holy Spirit'. The ministrant of the sacrament is the priest, but in necessity a deacon or lay person may baptize providing they use the forms above and intend to do what the church effects.

This way of thinking continued in the church after the Reformation, thus in the Book of Common Prayer the minister, in the event of some question about a child being lawfully baptized, is to ask the questions, 'by whom was the child baptized?', 'with what matter was this child baptized?' and 'with what words was this child baptized?' The prayer book directs the priest in the case of any doubt in this area to conduct a conditional baptism 'if you are not already baptized, I baptize you . . .'

There was considerable debate about the minister of baptism. The Council of Florence said that it was a parish priest under normal circumstances but that lay people baptized in necessity. This tradition was continued in the Reformation, and the books of common prayer take the same position, lay baptism is valid.

These may seem abstract questions but they are relevant in mission and pastoral work. A person presents themselves from a different Christian group to your own as a baptized person who wishes to become a part of the group and receive Holy Communion. What do you do in terms of receiving, say, an Armenian, or somebody from an Oriental church (the issue presenting itself in the thirteenth century) or today from a Gnostic Church in California, or a Mormon, or a Jehovah's Witness? Suddenly, in this context, bits of theology from the fifteenth century become important.

Sarum

The Sarum rite was the most commonly used of the medieval rites in England.[16] It may come as a surprise that there was not complete liturgical uniformity, but there were other local variations, based around Hereford, Bangor, York and Lincoln.

The Sarum rite is a variation on the Roman rite, with influences from Rouen. In 1078 Osmond was made Bishop of Salisbury, a part of the Norman policy of removing the Anglo-Saxon episcopate. He began to revise the liturgical books including the breviary and manuals, and these began to be used in southern England and Ireland. The Sarum rite is important because it is the service that Cranmer and most of his companions would have used in their younger life, and it is the rite from which the Book of Common Prayer derives some of its material.

The context of Sarum is of a Christian country in which there are virtually no adult baptisms. Thus the rite is performed in one ceremony, beginning with catechumenal rites, then baptism, and post-baptismal actions. What was once spread over a number of weeks has been now compressed together. The following table indicates the order of the service.

Table 1 The Sarum rite

The order for making a catechumenate	
Signing of the forehead, breast and right hand	This section of the rite is conducted at the door of the church.
Prayer for the candidate	
Prayer for protection with the cross	
Exorcism of salt	
Salt placed in mouth	
Prayer to hunger for salvation	
Prayer to send an angel to guard them *	The prayers marked with an * have different forms for male and female candidates.
Adjuration of the devil *	
Prayer for the reception of the candidate *	
Adjuration of the devil *	
Exorcism *	
Adjuration repeating previous prayer *	
Prayer for illumination	The priest makes the sign of the cross on the forehead.

Exorcism of candidate	
Reading from Gospel of Matthew	
Effeta	Opening of the ears and nose by use of saliva.
Recitation of Lord's Prayer, Hail Mary, and Apostles' Creed	
Sign of the cross on right hand	
Blessing	
Leading catechumenate by right hand	At this point the candidates are led into the church.
Blessing of the font	A full form is given but it is clear that the water was left in the font and therefore this blessing did not occur at every service.
Address to the godparents	
Litany of the saints	
Prayer for effectual ministry	
Blessing of the water	This is a long and complex prayer which includes the actions of making a cross in the water, casting the water in four directions, breathing on the water in the form of a cross, dropping some candle wax into the font, and dividing the water with the candle in the form of a cross.
Pouring holy oil in the water	
Pouring chrism in the water	
Pouring the two oils together in order	
Baptism	
Renunciation of Satan	
Anointing with holy oil	
Profession of faith	
Questioning of desire	
Baptism	The infant is dipped three times in the water.
Chrismation	

Dressing in chrismal robe (the chrisom)	
Giving of a candle	
	The rubrics direct immediate confirmation if a bishop is present.
Exhortation to godparents	An optional reading from Mark may be added as a protection against epilepsy.
Reading from Gospel of John	
	There are now a considerable number of directions for the priest in teaching people about baptism and confirmation.
Confirmation	This happens not as a part of baptism but later.
Versicle and responses	
Prayer for the sevenfold spirits	
Consignation	Bishop anoints his thumb with chrism and makes the sign of the cross on the forehead.
Prayer for the candidate	
Versicle and response	
Blessing	

While the rite still includes elements of the catechumenate, done outside the church and then baptism inside, it has now separated out confirmation, which only occurs if the bishop is present. There is now no expectation that the candidates will receive Holy Communion. Instead there are a considerable number of rubrics which direct the priest to exhort parents to bring their children for confirmation and then be admitted to Holy Communion. Thus all the elements of the rite are similar to much that we have seen earlier, for example *Ordo Romanus* 11, but the actual way that the rite is conducted has now split the baptismal liturgy into a variety of actions: baptism, confirmation, Holy Communion. This appears to deny that baptism is full initiation and raises the question of what confirmation is for. This latter question plagued the late medieval church and continues to be a problem within Anglicanism.

Postscript

The medieval church developed a variety of baptismal approaches in a complex mission situation. In many places there was a change from adult baptism to infant baptism, except where there was continued encounter with unevangelized tribes. In many places candidates, now infants, were fully initiated by allowing all actions to be done by the local presbyter. In Rome various post-baptismal ceremonies were reserved to the bishop. This practice spread because of the influence and respect for Rome. This was the pattern inherited in England at the Reformation. Mission had become directed to the next generation where all lived within a Christian society. This too continued in initial Reformation conceptions of Church and society.

Notes

1 E. C. Whitaker, 1960, *Documents of the Baptismal Liturgy*, London: SPCK, pp. 154–8.

2 Whitaker, *Documents*, pp. 166–96.

3 Whitaker, *Documents*, pp. 231–53.

4 Catholic Church, 1994, *Catechism of the Catholic Church*, London: Geoffrey Chapman, para. 1250.

5 Church of England, 1662, 1982, The Book of Common Prayer, Cambridge: Cambridge University Press, pp. 263–4.

6 Book of Common Prayer, p. 615.

7 Church of England, 1980, *The Alternative Service Book*, Cambridge: Cambridge University Press, p. 280, para 106.

8 The Liturgy is the name used for Holy Communion in Eastern Orthodox Churches.

9 T. C. Akeley, 1967, *Christian Initiation in Spain, c. 300–1100*, London: Darton, Longman & Todd.

10 Whitaker, *Documents*, pp. 117–22.

11 Whitaker, *Documents*, pp. 33–52.

12 Whitaker, *Documents*, pp. 213–21.

13 Thomas M. Finn, 1992, *Early Christian Baptism and the Catechumenate: Italy, North Africa, and Egypt*, Collegeville: Liturgical Press, pp. 77–9.

14 J. D. C. Fisher, 1965, *Christian Initiation: Baptism in the Medieval West*, Alcuin Club Collection 47, London: SPCK.

15 Whitaker, *Documents*, pp. 196–204.

16 Whitaker, *Documents*, pp. 231–53.

4

Reformation: Infant Baptism and Mission

While the break with Rome occurred under the reign of Henry VIII, there was no significant Reformation in his time. The change came with his son Edward VI who, as a minor, was under the influence of Protestant lord protectors. Archbishop Thomas Cranmer viewed this through the lens of the story of Josiah, the minor-age king of Israel who led a purification of worship under the influence of Hilkiah the high priest (2 Kings 22). Cranmer was able to reform the worship and this came in a succession of books of common prayer, one in 1549 and a more radical one in 1552. Under Mary a counter-reformation occurred and the Sarum rite was restored, though the religious policy made her very unpopular. With Elizabeth, Protestantism was restored and a very minimally modified 1552 book was used. This continued in use until the Commonwealth, when in 1645 the prayer book was made illegal.[1] With the return of the king a revision of the liturgy occurred and the 1662 Book of Common Prayer was produced, which stands as one of the official service books for the Church of England today.

The Book of Common Prayer

Cranmer's first revision in 1549 continued the trends that had been happening in the Western Church in terms of baptismal rites. At this point in history the mission of the Church was to the nation and thus the concern was with the bringing up of the next generation in the Christian faith. Thus the only service of baptism in the 1549 prayer book was a service of infant baptism and there was no provision for the baptism of adults; it simply did not happen.

Another factor in being a Church for the nation was uniformity in worship. We have already seen that the Sarum rite was one of the rites used in England (and we should note that the Church of England included in this period dioceses in Wales), but there was not uniformity within the nation. The Book of Common Prayer was designed to bring that uniformity, which had become possible through the advent of the printing press. Technological advance had enabled a greater consistency in liturgical provision. This technological factor was not to change significantly until the advent of the home computer.

One obvious thing to state concerning the new prayer books was that they were in English. Up until that point the language for worship was Latin. The Sarum rite was conducted in Latin, with occasional questions in English where necessary. Clearly some people were fluent in Latin and others understood it, but for many people it was an unknown language. Cranmer was concerned that the people should understand their worship. The Bible in English was put in every parish church, and then the prayer book arrived to help people worship in English. This did not exclude the use of other languages, as there were translations into Latin for worship in the universities, and into Welsh (1551), and then into French for the Channel Islands and Calais (1553). There was also a musical edition by Merbecke in 1550. This was a change in mission strategy, where understanding in worship was made central, as was worship in a way that fostered biblical literacy, not only through long readings from Scripture, but also through the very text of the prayers reflecting the biblical story.

If the early Church had seen a proliferation of secondary symbols around the primary symbol of baptism, the Reformation was to see a reverse process with the reduction in secondary symbols, primarily in order to show the centrality of baptism itself. In 1549 some secondary symbols were kept: signing with the cross, exorcism, the white robe and anointing. In 1552 these are swept way, save for the signing with the cross, which is moved to after baptism, and this proved to be contentious with the Puritans who wanted it abolished.

Table 2 Baptism in the books of common prayer

1549	1552	1662
Introduction	Introduction	Introduction
Flood prayer	Flood prayer	Flood prayer
Signing with cross		
Prayer	Prayer	Prayer
Exorcism		
Mark 10	Mark 10	Mark 10
Exhortation	Exhortation	Exhortation
Lord's Prayer	Prayer	Prayer
Apostles' Creed		
Entry into church		
Address to godparents	Address to godparents	Address to godparents
Renunciation	Renunciation	Renunciation
Creed in question form, 3 questions	Creed in question form, 1 question	Creed in question form, 1 question
	Prayer for candidates	Prayer over water
Baptism	Baptism	Baptism
	Signing with cross	Signing with cross
White robe		
Anointing		
	'Seeing now . . .'	'Seeing now . . .'
	Lord's Prayer	Lord's Prayer
	Thanksgiving	Thanksgiving
Exhortation	Exhortation	Exhortation

The 1549 services

In constructing the 1549 service of public baptism Cranmer used the Sarum baptismal rite and a Lutheran source, Hermann's *Consultation*. Cranmer kept some of the shape of the Sarum rite in

1549, with the first part of the service being held in the church porch and drawing on elements of the ancient catechumenate. The introductory rubric comments that there were two times a year when baptism used to be performed, Easter and Whitsuntide, but this is a custom that has gone out of use. Nevertheless the service is one of public baptism and it is expected that this occur after matins with a congregation present.

The introduction begins by explaining that we are born in sin but that Jesus Christ came in bounteous mercy that we might be baptized with the Spirit. The flood prayer, as it is called, it is taken from Hermann, looks at God's plan of salvation history through the ark, the crossing of the Red Sea, and Jesus baptism, and prays that this might be a 'laver of regeneration' (Gen. 6–9; Ex. 14; Mark 1; and Titus 3.4–7). The child is then named and signed with the cross on his or her forehead and breast, being told not to be ashamed of faith in Christ crucified. The following prayer asks for the spiritual regeneration of the child. Then comes the exorcism: 'I command of thee, unclean spirit in the name of the Father, and of the Son, and of the Holy Ghost, that thou come out and depart . . .' Exorcism had been a large part in catechumenate rites, but this was now reduced to a single exorcism, in common with the Lutheran churches of the continent. The service continues with the reading from Mark 10.13–16 ('Suffer the little children to come to me') and an exhortation to faith that God will answer our prayers in baptism. The godparents then recite the Lord's Prayer and the Apostles' Creed, elements of which are derived from ceremonies in the catechumenate. The first part of the service ends with a prayer for the candidates and then the children are taken into church, led by the right hand.

The second part of the service exhorts the godparents to faith and then proceeds with a threefold renunciation of evil and a threefold declaration of faith. The rubrics make it clear that the priest is talking to the child and the godparents are answering on their behalf. The child is then baptized with a threefold dipping in the water. Post-baptismal ceremonies include the giving of a white robe and anointing with holy oil. The final act is an exhortation to the godparents that the child be brought up in the Christian faith. 'These children have promised by you' to follow Christ and you are to help them in learning Christian basics. So there is clearly an expectation of the mission of the Church to be taken on by the laity in their families. The rubrics also mention further instruction in the catechism.

The second service in the 1549 prayer book is 'of them that be baptized in private houses in time of necessity'. It gives directions as to how people may baptize at home in an emergency. It then goes on to give directions for a service in the church for the reception of that child 'into Christ's true flock', using elements of the previous service. There is also a form of conditional baptism, if the baptized status of the infant is in some doubt. Finally, this section includes a prayer for the blessing of the water. In Sarum it was not the practice to bless water at each baptism, and Cranmer here has continued the same practice, providing a prayer over the water but not to be used at each service. This includes a fairly strong epiclesis on the water:

> Send down we beseech thee the same thy holy spirit to assist us, and to be present at this our invocation of thy holy name: Sanctify + this fountain of baptism, thou that art the sanctifier of all things, that by the power of thy word, all those that shall be baptized therein, may be spiritually regenerated.[2]

These two services were seen to be sufficient for a reformed Church of England.

Martin Bucer, one of the continental reformers who had taken temporary refuge in England, wrote a book called the *Censura* which made comments on all the services in the 1549 prayer book.[3] He much approved of baptism being a public service and welcomed the statement at the beginning of the service to that end. He wished to abolish the use of the white robe and chrism, acknowledging that both were ancient ceremonies but questioning whether they encouraged greater reverence. He suggested that not everyone who comes to baptism is demonically possessed and would have preferred instead a prayer of protection. Finally, he disliked the consecration of the baptismal water, mostly from a fear of superstition, which he saw as potentially in opposition to the building up of faith.

The 1552 services

In 1552 Cranmer further simplified the service. The service was now held completely in the church, by the font. Rather than modify the exorcism Cranmer removes it completely, and puts the signing of the cross after baptism. The recitation of the creed and the Lord's Prayer by the godparents is now omitted and the renunciation turned into one question, as is the question of belief, using the Apostles' Creed. The petitions at the end of the blessing of the font are now reduced to four short prayers for the candidate. This is followed by a further prayer for the candidate. The signing with the cross now follows baptism and a new statement by the priest is included, exhorting people to thanksgiving since the child 'is now regenerate' and grafted into Christ's body (Titus 3.4–7; Rom. 11.11–24). As with the previous book there is a final rubric that the child should learn the catechism and be brought to the bishop for confirmation.

The service of private baptism follows the 1549 book, adopting any changes made to the public service, and omitting ceremonies that had now been abolished. Also excluded is the blessing of the water of the font, which is simply omitted in the 1552 book. Perhaps Cranmer took on Bucer's comment about the danger of superstition, and the doubt that there was any real benefit to faith in suggesting some sort of change in the water.

The 1662 services

In 1662 the prayer book was revised with a new start for the Church of England after the Commonwealth period. The infant baptism service closely followed the 1552 service but with a number of revisions. It omitted the statement about baptism being in Easter and Whitsuntide. This is unfortunate as it finally cut the connection with potential baptismal seasons. The 1662 service became the archetypal Church of England Prayer Book, still in use today. It added in the rubrics at the beginning that no minister may refuse baptism save for the purpose of preparation, and directed laity to contact the bishop if there are any problems. This may represent a reaction to some of the behaviours of pastors in the Commonwealth period. The preliminary part of the service follows 1552 very closely but there is some tidying up. For example, in the renunciation it is made clear that the answer is given, 'in the name of this child'. The prayer for the candidates immediately prior to baptism is changed into a prayer over the water: 'Sanctify this water to the mystical washing away of sin.' This clause is added and the end of the prayer modified in a move away from Bucer – one of a number of signs of the 1662 restorers recognizing the place of material objects in God's sacramental economy. This is in the context of a more mature consideration of the Reformation and the influence of Calvinistic theology, which emphasizes, in light of our weak faith, the need for God to help us and speak his promise to us through material elements such as water, bread and wine. The exhortation at the end of the service has an extra paragraph added in 1662 where it is made quite clear that people are to learn the Apostles' Creed, the Lord's Prayer, and the ten commandments and then are to be taken to the bishop to be confirmed. Again this may have been a necessary addition after the Commonwealth period, during which episcopacy had been abolished. Indeed, we know that with the return of the king, the bishops began their work of confirmation in earnest.[4] The service finishes with a rubric justifying the signing of the cross in baptism.

The directions for private baptism follow the changes in the 1662 book. However a new context now arose through the migration of large numbers of Anglicans to live in colonies overseas. It took some time to build churches so baptism was more often ministered privately at home. Indeed there was quite a struggle to bring baptism back into the church.

The catechism

The first two books of Common Prayer have the catechism and the service of confirmation together as one service. Nowadays it is common to ignore the catechism as an outmoded way of instruction. It is a Reformation feature of the prayer book that the catechism is included. This was something particularly developed by the Lutherans and then included in the Church of England. The first catechism centred around the three texts of the Apostles' Creed, the Lord's Prayer and the ten commandments. In 1604 an addition was made to the catechism adding a section explaining the sacraments.

It should be noted that the prevailing theological paradigm of the period was Calvinism. God approaches us by covenants; these are works of his grace. Each covenant has covenant signs, both of initiation and renewal. The signs are important because of the weakness of our faith and are effectual signs of God's promise. The sign of initiation in the old covenant was circumcision, in the new covenant it is baptism. Baptism assures the parents of God's gracious favour to their children and stirs up faith in the congregation reasserting God's unmerited favour in Jesus Christ. In drawing a theologically based parallel by covenant between old and new it is easier to maintain infant baptism as biblical, both covenants being open to children. By rooting all sacraments in God's promise it is theologically viable to have the reading 'suffer the little children come to me' as a reading at infant baptism, as it speaks of God's promise of grace, the very thing the water sign is proclaiming. Hence the catechism begins with the assertion of the effect of baptism:

> My Baptism: wherein I was made a member of Christ, the child of God, and an inheritor of the kingdom of heaven.[5]

Moderate international Calvinism prevailed, even if you were an Arminian (being a reaction to strict Calvinism), through the seventeenth and eighteenth centuries. Baptism was the beginning of the covenant of grace.

The three texts – the ten commandments, Lord's Prayer and Apostles' Creed – have been central to catechetical teaching throughout the whole history of the Church in England. Many other people developed further catechisms to explain in more detail particular areas of doctrine. One particularly important catechism was that written by Alexander Nowell (Dean of St Paul's during much of the reign of Elizabeth I). Indeed, alongside the official catechism all manner of catechisms developed.[6]

The sacramental addition to the catechism has given Anglicanism some positive teaching on the sacraments which is so important that it is worth quoting here.

> How many Sacraments hath Christ ordained in his church?
> Two only, as generally necessary to salvation; that it is to say, Baptism, and the Supper of the Lord.
> What meanest thou by this word Sacrament?
> I mean an outward and visible sign of an inward and spiritual grace given to us, ordained by Christ himself, as a means whereby we receive the same, and a pledge to assure us thereof.[7]

This has become a standard Anglican way of looking at a sacrament. It then distinguishes between the outward sign and the inward grace and applies this to baptism.

> What is the outward visible sign or form in baptism?
> Water: wherein the person is baptized, in the name of the Father, and of the Son, and of the Holy Ghost.
> What is the inward and spiritual grace?
> A death unto sin, and a new birth unto righteousness: for being by nature born in sin, and the children of wrath, we are hereby made the children of grace.[8]

Thus for many years Anglicans were taught basic doctrine and Christian lifestyle.

Clergy were exhorted in a variety of ways to be involved in catechetical work, through injunctions, visitation reports and various other methods of inspection. Indeed, in the eighteenth century, catechetical work was greatly developed, as we shall see in our discussion of Anglican mission. It certainly played a major part in shaping the Christian life of many, and as such was a part of the mission of the Church in deepening the Christian lives of those baptized.

Confirmation

Many of the reformers abolished confirmation, particularly in the Reformed tradition. Children were catechized and then admitted to communion without any ceremony on a quarterly communion day.[9] This practice happened in the Channel Islands where, before 1818, no bishop had travelled for confirmation. The register of St Clement's Parish, Jersey, records the number of young people admitted to communion from 1697 to 1772.[10] It was clear that this happened at quarterly communions. Some Lutherans and the Church of England, however, kept confirmation. In the Cranmerian prayer books it is a service tacked onto the end of the catechism. In 1662 it stands as a separate service in its own right.

We have seen that the Roman tradition was to reserve the episcopal rites at the end of the Easter baptism service to the bishop. Thus they were only performed with the bishop present or done separately later. The English prayer books have taken this direction logically forward and made confirmation a stand-alone service. Calvin justified not giving communion to children on the basis of Paul's comments in 1 Corinthians 11.29 about the importance of 'discerning the body'. Until such time as they could understand what they were doing and come with a prepared heart it was thought that children should not receive communion. Part of that preparation was a basic Christian catechizing. So those who were baptized as infants had to come to confirmation in order to renew the solemn vow made in their name at their baptism. This is the internal logic of the prayer book confirmation services and as such is a part of a mission strategy to the country.

The services of confirmation are laid out in the table below.

Table 3 Services of confirmation

1549	1552	1662
		{Catechism}
Catechism	Catechism	
		Introduction
		Ratification of baptismal vow
Versicles and greeting	Versicles and greeting	Versicles and greeting
Isaiah 11.2 prayer	Isaiah 11.2 prayer	Isaiah 11.2 prayer
Prayer		
Signing and hand laying	Hand laying	Hand laying
Pax		Greeting
		Lord's Prayer
Prayer	Prayer	Prayers – 2
Blessing	Blessing	Blessing
Rubric	Rubric	Rubric

The 1549 service has removed any application of unction (oil) but does pray for an inward work of the Holy Spirit. The candidates are signed with the sign of the cross and have hands laid on them, keeping much of the medieval form. In 1552 this is swept away and a new prayer introduced ('Defend O Lord this child with thy heavenly grace') as the prayer for confirmation. The 1662 service was strengthened by making clear that there was a ratification of baptismal vows. John Cosin, Bishop of Durham, 1660–72, who was involved in revising the service wanted an even longer form with a ministry of the Word and several questions both about renunciation and belief.[11] So the service became a prayer of strengthening for those who had been baptized as infants, and a necessary part of their spiritual development.

It was not the practice to have a confirmation service with Holy Communion. Bishops tended to hold confirmations in the summer. For a long period communion was quarterly and there might be a long gap between being confirmed and actually receiving communion. This was thought by some to be an opportunity for further catechizing.[12]

So far we have looked at a mission strategy of baptizing the nation and teaching the children so they will grow to Christian adulthood. As such, confirmation makes pastoral sense. However, the initiation of adults had already become a part of English mission, with the rise of Quakers and Baptists who converted to the Church of England needing baptism. This implicitly raised questions about the nature and necessity of confirmation. These questions were to become very acute in the twentieth century, which we will come to later. It also has to be remembered that adults who were baptized were often admitted to communion on the basis of being 'ready and desirous' of confirmation, in accordance with the rubric of the Book of Common Prayer. Indeed, there is evidence to suggest that those who had been admitted to communion were then regarded as not needing confirmation.[13]

Mission and rites of transfer

One aspect of church growth is called transfer growth; when a Christian moves from one church to another. In the period we are now looking at there are at least two examples of such transference, both involving force or persecution in a conversion process. The first is of people who were forcibly converted to Islam and then brought back to the Christian faith. The second is of people who through times of persecution converted to Catholicism. In both cases rites were provided in order to bring them back to the Christian faith, or the Church of England. The first had a clear baptismal element to it. The second begins a process which will eventually be included in *Common Worship: Christian Initiation*.

Reconciliation of an apostate

In the seventeenth century there was considerable trouble with pirates in the Mediterranean. These were slave traders from North Africa and merchant ships travelling through those waters were in danger; indeed at one point one village in Cornwall was attacked and people were kidnapped. On being taken captive they were sold into slavery and forcibly converted to Islam or killed. Some would manage to escape and others would be ransomed by their relatives. On return most wished to reconvert to Christianity. In 1637 Archbishop Laud composed a liturgy for these circumstances. This is not a well-known piece of mission history and was resolved in the end by a violent attack on one of the centres of this activity making clear that Britain was unwilling to accept this piracy.[14]

Laud's rite was called 'A form of penance and reconciliation of a renegado or apostate from the Christian religion to turkism'. As such it is a curious and sad admittance of how bad were interfaith relationships. The first stage in the process of reconversion was to go to the bishop and be excommunicated. The excommunication would then be read out both in the cathedral and parish church. After a conference with the minister a series of penitential actions would occur. On the first Sunday the penitent would stand dressed in a white sheet with a white wand in their hand at the church door and ask the people who passed by to pray for them. On the second Sunday, in the same attire, they were brought into the church to the font where they would confess that they had sinned and ask to be restored. They kissed the bottom stone of the font and struck their breast before departing. On the third Sunday they were to stand in the body of the church near the minister's view in penitential habit and were exhorted to repentance. They then publicly confessed the sin of renouncing the Saviour and asked for pardon. The priest then came forth and used an adaptation of the absolution in the Book of Common Prayer service for the sick, including the phrase 'I absolve thee from this thy heinous crime of renegation'. The priest then knelt down and prayed for the penitent. After that the minister raised them to their feet, took away the white sheet and wand, and exhorted them to prove themselves in all holy obedience. They were then told that they may receive Holy Communion at the next communion day and should make an oblation (that is, an offering) according to their ability.

It should be said that excommunications did occur in the seventeenth and eighteenth centuries, often for sexual irregularity.

However there were sufficient numbers of people coming back from North Africa who wished to reconvert to Christianity for this service to be a necessity. The penitential habit was used in other excommunications, but often a simple form of confession was sufficient for restoration. Here is a more elaborate service. In the symbolic acts that the penitent had to make, there is a clear connection to baptism. The penitent stood at the font and confessed their sins. At the font they asked God to forgive this heinous and horrible sin and be restored to the benefit of this sacrament which they had wickedly abjured. They then kissed the foot of the font. The service was taking the penitent back to their baptismal promises and directing them to confess and then go forward in faith.

Adjurations in Jersey

For many years the French Reformed Church was terribly persecuted by the Roman Catholics in France. This aroused much sympathy in the Church of England, and was a pastorally significant issue in the Channel Islands, where many French Protestants fled in order to escape persecution. The register in St Clement's Church in Jersey between 1697 and 1702 records 21 adjurations which happened at the quarterly services.[15] Because of persecution some people had converted to Catholicism, but on managing to escape France they wished to renounce the Catholic faith and confess their Protestant convictions. These types of services happened in other Huguenot settings on the mainland in places such as Southampton and London. There was not a rite as such but a pastoral context in which people would renounce Catholicism and retake the Protestant faith.

Postscript

This chapter has concentrated on the baptism of children and the accompanying rites leading to Christian maturity. It has then begun to look at the beginnings of approaches to the transfer of people between denominations and between religions. This last part is an indication of the change of culture going on around the Church of England. England was increasingly in a wider world with missionary possibilities.

The Reformation continued the trends of medieval liturgy. Thus services were composed for children only, confirmation was separated as an adjunct to catechism, and finally as a stand-alone service. In order to sustain Christian discipleship, catechisms were introduced as a new way of forming children in faith. The one service that has been omitted from this chapter is the new service that was introduced in 1662, a form of service for the baptism of those who were 'of riper years'. The inclusion of this service in the seventeenth century is an indication of the changing culture, and of the widening horizons of the British people. Therefore I want to start Chapter 5 with this service and then look at adult baptism and world mission in Anglicanism.

Notes

1 G. J. Cuming, 1969, *A History of Anglican Liturgy*, London: Macmillan.

2 Church of England, 1910, 1938, *The First and Second Prayer Books of Edward VI*, Everyman's Library 448, London: J. M. Dent, p. 245.

3 E. C. Whitaker, 1974, *Martin Bucer and the Book of Common Prayer*, Alcuin Club Collection No. 55, Great Wakering: Mayhew–McCrimmon.

4 Phillip Tovey, 2014, *Anglican Confirmation: 1662–1820*, Farnham: Ashgate.

5 Church of England, 1662, 1968, *The Book of Common Prayer*, Cambridge: Cambridge University Press, p. 289.

6 I. M. Green, 1996, *The Christian's ABC: Catechism and Catechizing in England*, Oxford: Oxford University Press.

7 Book of Common Prayer, p. 294.

8 Book of Common Prayer, pp. 294–5.

9 Hughes Oliphant Old, 1992, *The Shaping of the Reformed Baptismal Rite in the Sixteenth Century*, Grand Rapids: Eerdmans.

10 See Philip Tovey, *Eighteenth Century Anglican Confirmation: Renewing the Covenant of Grace*, Joint Liturgical Study (forthcoming).

11 Tovey, *Anglican Confirmation: 1662-1820*.

12 Tovey, *Anglican Confirmation: 1662–1820*.

13 Tovey, *Anglican Confirmation: 1662–1820*.

14 W. Laud, 1695, *Annual Accounts of the Province Presented to the King*, London: Chitwell, pp. 372–6.

15 Jersey Archive, Composite Register St Clement's Church, G/C.07/A1/2. See also Philip Tovey, 2015, *Eighteenth-Century Anglican Confirmation: Renewing the Covenant of Grace*, Norwich: Canterbury Press, pp. 37–46.

5

Adult Baptism and World Mission in Anglicanism

In 1662 a new service was added to the prayer book: 'The ministration of baptism to such as are of ripe years and are able to answer for themselves'. It was basically a rite of adult baptism. This was needed for a number of reasons. In England the rise of Quakers and Baptists during the Commonwealth period meant that the previous policy of baptizing the nation had ceased and clergy were confronted with young adults who were unbaptized. Through migration, particularly to the colonies in North America, laity and clergy had come in contact with native American peoples and had begun some work of evangelization. While there is a woeful tale of wars with the native people, there is a less well-known story of mission work done by Anglicans which entailed the baptism of adults. There is also the shameful story of slavery in the Caribbean and the southern states of America, and though some owners were reluctant, others allowed their slaves to become Christians. Once again adults needed baptism. Migration and mission was to be one of the factors in the life of the Church of England. This was to develop into full-scale mission both through overseas chaplains and then through missionary societies. This chapter will look at issues of world evangelization and baptism, and its influence on the liturgy.

Baptism for those able to answer for themselves

'The public baptism of such as are of riper years' was accepted by convocation in 1661 and added to the prayer book which went to parliament for approval in 1662. It was included because of the pastoral need. It was based on the service of infant baptism, but with a whole string of minor changes to adjust it to the context of a person who could speak for themselves. Thus the questions are directed to the candidate; the godparents are there as sponsors and witnesses. The Bible reading was changed to that of the visit of Nicodemus to Jesus in John's Gospel (John 3), reflecting an adult conversation about entering the kingdom of heaven. The rubrics exhorted the minister to instruct the candidate and required that notice should be given to the bishop. The candidate is exhorted at the end to godly living.

The final rubric says:

> It is expedient that every person, thus baptized, should be confirmed by the bishop so soon after his baptism as conveniently may be; that so he may be admitted to the Holy Communion.[1]

While this may have been the desire, the practice was of confirmation every three years with a visitation of the diocese by the bishop as required by canon. This could lead to a gap between the baptism and the possibility of confirmation. In the eighteenth century the baptism of adults was a regular occurrence (though the total number baptized was relatively small), and some were admitted to communion without confirmation. There was a clear belief by some bishops that, once admitted to communion, confirmation was not required.[2]

It is unfortunate that convocation did not spend more time considering the matter of adult baptism, perhaps because it was seen as a quick response to a pastoral problem that may have been expected to be eradicated in the next few years. The fact that the liturgy was based on infant baptism is a reversal of the previous pattern. We have seen so far that liturgies were written assuming the evangelization of adults, and primarily for adults, with children being included in a secondary and concessionary way. Here there is an inversion of this historical pattern, with the rites for children being the model for the rite for adults. This is a highly unsatisfactory approach and it is unfortunate that the Church of England did not rectify this issue until after the Second World War! The mission expansion of the Church of England and other parts of Anglicanism was to lead to adult baptism being of significance in non-Christian contexts where adults would be the primary candidates for baptism, as they are in some parts of the world today.

Catechetical strategies in a new world

The reformed Church of England took catechizing quite seriously and developed it considerably. The question and answer form was widely used and, in conjunction with the official catechism itself, all manner of catechisms developed, including Nowell's catechism and Robert Nelson's catechetical approach to the feasts and festivals of the Church of England.[3] Alongside these catechisms there were commentaries written on the catechism which were used in producing catechetical lectures. These were done by a wide variety of people of different approaches and included books by the orthodox Thomas Bray, Samuel Clarke a key latitudinarian, and Archbishop Thomas Secker (who was keen on catechizing).[4] These books were both studies to be read by people privately, and manuals for clergy in their catechizing work. Indeed the teaching of the catechism was not left just to clergy, but could also be the responsibility of schoolteachers employed by the Church, and overseas catechists both taught the catechism and led morning and evening prayer.

After the Commonwealth it was clear that Anglicans wished to have more than the simple parrot recital of the catechism. Bray came to fame for writing a commentary on the catechism. It was intended to be in two volumes and was never completed, only the first volume being published. However, Bray is a significant character because not only was he the rector in an influential city church, but he also helped found the SPCK and the SPG, and had a hands-on approach to recruiting and supporting people sent out to the colonies to do the Church's work.

The first focus of this was in the colonies in North America. He had been a commissary of the Bishop of London to Maryland in 1696, where he conducted a visitation for the bishop. He then wrote a report on the needs of the Church in America in which he suggested that there needed to be 51 more ministers, 20 of whom were needed for work with the 'native Indians'.

The SPG wrote a manual for missionaries based on Bray's work, called *The Instructions for Missionaries*. This included regular catechizing, particularly towards the reception of Holy Communion. It advised that children's catechizing be divided into three groups:

> Under 9 years old – where they are to learn by heart the catechism and morning and evening prayer;
> Between 9 and 13 – where they are to learn some exposition of the catechism with scriptural proofs;
> Above 13 where they are to read edifying books, hold meetings on the Lord's Day, and learn the singing psalms.

This was a fairly comprehensive catechetical approach, but was not, as yet, to fully respond to the needs of the adult candidate, for in the colonies the native Americans were a part of his concern, and they would be adult candidates.

Thus catechizing was a significant aspect of the work of the Church. While this was not always as comprehensive as Bray envisaged, neither was it totally neglected. Some bishops were highly zealous in this area, for example, Secker, who would chase his clergy if he thought they were lax. This was a mission strategy designed for baptized children but also used for unbaptized adults, to teach the basics of the Christian faith in preparation for baptism and confirmation, or for confirmation. In the eighteenth century some held that to neglect confirmation was to neglect the covenant made in baptism, and thus possibly to lose your salvation.[5]

New thoughts on baptism in England and Scotland

While there was very little liturgical change after 1662 until the beginning of the twentieth century, that does not mean that there were not significant suggestions for change, and attempts at it. In general there are two trends: one is in a patristic direction and the other is towards simplification. The groups involved were, on the one hand the Nonjurors, including the Scottish bishops, and on the other Latitudinarians and evangelicals.

With the Glorious Bloodless Revolution of 1688 clergy were faced with having to take a new oath to the king while the old (deposed) king was alive. This produced a crisis within the Church, one of such a magnitude that perhaps has not been seen since, in that the Archbishop of Canterbury himself left the Church of England, to become a Nonjuror. It also left the Scottish bishops in the difficult position of being asked to support a foreign king against the Stuart king.

The *Apostolic Constitutions*, an early Church order, were seen as a significant document, not least because some argued for their apostolicity. The Nonjurors showed a keen interest in liturgy looking at the earlier prayer books, particularly the 1549 book, and studying Eastern Orthodox rites and patristic writings. This bore fruit in Thomas Deacon's book of *Devotions*. In it he reintroduced the form of admitting a catechumen and added exorcisms from 1549 to the baptismal rites, and anointing in baptism and confirmation from Anglican and Orthodox sources. The Scottish bishops at the same time introduced anointing in confirmation (but confirmations were quite rare in Scotland) and the blessings of oils from Orthodox sources. While of liturgical interest, these were in fact quite small groups, but they prefigure some of what was to happen later.

William Whiston, while not a part of these groups, and certainly a highly eccentric figure, in 1713 produced *The Liturgy of the Church of England Reduced nearer to the Primitive Standard*. This was a combination of baptism and confirmation with prayers added from *Apostolic Constitutions*. What became clear is that the rite is for older children who can speak for themselves and adults, as Whiston himself did not baptize babies. He remained in the Church of England for over 30 years before he became a Baptist.

Samuel Clarke is one of the figures that tower over the Latitudinarian clergy. These were the clergy who had been influenced by the Enlightenment within England, the key figures being Newton and Locke. Clarke privately made suggestions for change in the liturgy, making handwritten annotations of the Book of Common Prayer, but these were not published in his lifetime, although known to a few. A number of people in this party, some of whom were to become Unitarian, produced proposed books of common prayer. The trend was to remove the language of regeneration and replace it with joining the Church, to simplify the service, often by the removal of the renunciation of the devil, to remove the blessing of the water, and removing the sign of the cross. In confirmation there was a tendency to try to make this an adult rite at an older age of commitment. This trend can be seen in the proposed American prayer book (1786), which is perhaps a good example of Latitudinarian liturgical proposals of an orthodox theology, and in the so-called Franklin's Prayer Book (1773), which is less orthodox. The latter considerably reduces the rite of baptism, simply asking if people wish to be baptized and then performing the ceremony with an exhortation to virtuous Christian living.

The evangelical revival shared with Latitudinarianism a desire for simplification, as can be seen in John Wesley's *Sunday Service for Methodists in North America*.[6] Their contribution, however, is more significant in light of hymnody and the hymns they created on baptism. These mostly assume the baptism of children and put into song the petition for the effectual working of the sacrament that is found in the Book of Common Prayer. This can be illustrated by one verse from the *Collection of Hymns*:

Sealed with the baptismal seal,
Purchased by the atoning blood,
Jesus, in our children dwell,
Make the heart the house of God:
Fill thy consecrated shrine,
Father, Son, and Spirit divine.

Thus the hymn both looks to the objective atonement and prays for its effectual action through baptism. This outward action leading to an inward change is expressed perhaps more fully in a longer hymn which has a wider vision (quoting a selection of verses):

We now thy promised presence claim;
Sent to disciple all mankind,
Sent to baptize into thy name,
We now thy promised presence find.

Jesus, with us thou always art;
Effectual make the sacred sign,
The gift unspeakable impart,
And bless the ordinance divine

Eternal Spir't, descend from high,
Baptizer of our spirits thou!
The sacramental seal apply,
And witness with the water now.

The hymns are rich in baptismal theology. In returning to Matthew 28 they show the beginning of the world vision for mission. This was already implicit within the Church of England and something that the Evangelical movement picked up and fostered. However, they also show a clear embrace of sacramental theology and its pastoral application. This includes no division between the Spirit and the material, although focusing on internal change. The relationship between mission and baptism is not so clearly stated in any contemporary hymns.

The Anglicanism mission: liturgical and organizational implications

The worldwide development of Anglicanism at first through migration but then through evangelization required the reorganization of Anglican polity. The American Revolution led to the formation of a clearly independent Province. Going back to the principles of the Reformation provincial autonomy was asserted, and the possibility of an independent provincial liturgy. Thus the Protestant Episcopal Church of the United States of America had its own prayer book, and its own constitution, much more democratic than the Church of England at the time. While inviting the Church of England to comment on the proposed book, the final form was a completely American decision. The later history of the Anglican Communion, up to and beyond the first Lambeth Conference, is of the development of independent Provinces and a dispersed authority.

Liturgically the first phase was for the translation of the Bible and the Book of Common Prayer into various vernacular languages. Thus in North America the mission to the Mohawks led to a series of vernacular Books of Common Prayer, in the late eighteenth century. Broadly this was a fairly conservative translation with little liturgical innovation.[7] Thus even the title of baptism of those of riper years was often reproduced whereas it might have been simply labelled adult baptism.

Preaching, of course, could lead to amazing success, as happened with some of the people movements in South India.[8] Early mission work in South India was performed by Lutheran missionaries, but was to become a part of the Anglican Church. Evangelization by John Kolhoff led to the baptism of a Hindu who took the name David. He was sent to his home village in 1796 and began to preach the gospel. In 1797 baptisms began to occur and the whole village was gradually converted to Christianity. This led to opposition from neighbouring Hindu villages but other villages became Christian. Between April 1802 and January

1803 there were 46 services of baptism and 5,629 people were baptized. This put a great strain on the catechetical ability of the Church and eight years later some people reverted back to Hinduism. However Bishop Coldwell concludes that the problem was not premature baptism but neglected baptismal follow-up.[9] People movements might not have much liturgical implication, but they do have implications for the catechetical aspect of baptism and the organization of the local church, not least in the supply of teachers and ministers.

With the onset of the Oxford movement, and particularly ritualism, there came more liturgical innovation, and this was particularly true in areas where the Universities Mission to Central Africa (UMCA) was the primary mission. This could particularly be seen in Tanzania which at becoming a Province had one half following quite strictly the English prayer book and another part following independent high church traditions inherited from the UMCA. There is a huge corpus of prayer book translations and adaptations completed by the missionaries.

Catechumenal approaches

Some Anglican mission work of this period adopted a revised version of the catechumenate. This does not seem to have been systematically discussed as part of mission strategy but appears to have been incorporated into Anglican mission practice as part of preparation for adult baptism. This was extensively used around the world, as can be illustrated by a variety of quotes from missionary literature of the time. From this literature it can be seen that the approach was used both by the evangelical CMS and by the higher church SPG and UMCA. Gradually this developed liturgical expression, but it may well have come out of a pragmatic evangelization situation where those who began to respond needed to be prepared for baptism. Let us look at some examples from various regions.

Eugene Stock illustrates the growth of the work of CMS in China by reporting some of the statistics of the day.[10] In Fuh-kien he gives the following statistics:

Table 4 Church growth in Fuh-kien, 1882–94

	Catechumens	Baptized	Communicant
1882	2,000	2,400	1,300
1894	7,000	5,900	2,800

Stock is interested in showing the growth of the work in this province. However, what is shown is a mission strategy, in a non-Christian land, using the catechumenate as a way to prepare people for baptism, and then the need to prepare people after baptism for communion. Presumably the strategy includes a preparation for confirmation in order to gain communicant status. In that sense it is a modified strategy from the early Church.

In 1899 there was a conference of bishops of the Anglican Communion in China, Hong Kong and Korea; six were present.[11] In terms of order and discipline they made some interesting comments. The conference made a distinction between hearers and catechumens as stages towards becoming baptized as an adult. The hearers, the earliest stage, were to be admitted to the catechumenate by a special service sanctioned by the bishops. The catechumens were to be given special seats within the church to sit as a group. It was expected that during divine service there should be special prayers for the catechumens. Then the baptism of the catechumens should occur at key festivals, Christmas, Easter and Whitsuntide for example. Again there are some clear imitations of the catechumenate in the early Church as interpreted by Victorian missionaries.

The 1889 conference anticipated an 'Office for the Admission of Catechumens' printed in Korea in 1905.[12] The candidates stand at the door of the church and are asked to put away idols, evil spirits and sorcery, representing a rejection of some perceived aspects of traditional religion. Then they are asked to put away drunkenness and gluttony. This is followed by a determination to leave anger and quarrelling. Finally they are asked about their determination to learn the doctrines of the Christian faith. The minister then says:

> *N*, since you hope, with God's help, by a careful study and practice of the Doctrine, to receive baptism and to serve Him in His church to your life's end, I admit you as a catechumen.

The candidate is then signed with the sign of the cross. The final prayer asks for diligence in receiving instruction of the holy word and afterwards to be born again in baptism.

The annual report of the Melanesian mission in 1901 also gives some statistics and indication of mission strategy.[13] This mission also makes a distinction between hearers and catechumens, the former being unbaptized people who have come to church schools. Some indication of numbers is as follows.

Table 5 Church growth in Melanesia, 1901

	Hearers	Baptized	Communicants
Solomon Islands	1,192	5,642	1,016
New Hebrides	1,700	1,300	
Leper Island (for this year)	26	172	

The mission concludes that the hearers in total across all the islands is 4,459 and that there are 755 catechumens.

In southern Africa the catechumenate was already established before the Metropolitanate of Bishop Jones (1874–1908). Cecil Lewis and Gestrude Edwards illustrate some of the problems that the Church had to tackle, and in so doing illustrate part of the mission strategy. They describe what they saw as a repeated process. A mission station is set up with schools and medical facilities. It begins to set up outstations, and village elders ask for these in their village.

> Soon the large number of these dependent stations makes it impossible for one priest, in spite of the advent of a motor . . .

> to visit them often. The result is that many poorly instructed catechumens are baptized, confirmed, communicated, and instruct others. The priest cannot be the pastor of so large and scattered a flock, and they often cannot be fed. For the number of would-be Christians outstrip the resources of the Church to deal with them. By reorganization and development of training colleges for catechists and schoolmasters much has been done to remedy this.[14]

While this illustrates the problems, it also shows the strategy of building schools, colleges and medical work in order to commend the gospel to the people. There is also an assumption that the people will be trained as catechists and schoolmasters, and that both of these groups of people will be involved in propagating the Christian faith. Out of these hearers come the catechumens preparing for baptism, and then later those preparing for confirmation. We can see that this strategy was replicated across the world by Anglicans; indeed in South Africa the London Missionary Society (LMS) had a similar strategy, as was the case with other missionary societies.

It would be easy to give many further examples from different parts of the world. There was clearly the use of a catechumenate with native Americans in Canada and the United States, in central Africa and Madagascar, the Pacific islands including Hawaii, and Asia, in India, Singapore and Japan. Victorians not only preached the gospel, they took education and healthcare and used these in developing a Christian Church out of a non-Christian population.

In 1933 the SPG published a book *Worship in other Lands.*[15] This begins to consider the possibility of what would later be called inculturation, by describing various ceremonies and services. Included in the book are descriptions of the making of catechumens in India, Japan and southern Africa. This shows continuity with the mission work discussed above and also indicates that official forms had been developed for catechumens. These included the 1930 *Occasional Offices* in South Africa, the 1935 Melanesian *Catechism* which included prayers for those preparing for holy baptism, and the 1956 *Occasional Offices* in Nsenga in present-day Zambia. This latter rite is perhaps one of the most complex of Anglican pre-baptismal rites, which included the making of a catechumen (hanging a cross around their neck), the anointing of catechumens (with exorcism and the giving of the Lord's Prayer and creed), and a series of scrutinies in the week of baptism.[16]

Hearers gradually became catechumens; a transition that was ritualized. The catechumens were then baptized, often at major Christian festivals. Clearly the system was not perfect, as we have seen from the comments in southern Africa, and gradually it died out as the population was Christianized. This can be seen in Melanesia, where the mission reports increasingly indicated that the majority of the people on the islands had become Christian. At that point adult baptisms were expected to cease and infant baptisms become the norm. A repeat of earlier patterns of Christian history was occurring. But in other parts of the world Christians continued to remain a small minority, as say in Japan, China, or India; and elsewhere the Church has declined to a small body in a secular world. In those circumstances the catechumenate can still be a useful liturgical tool for mission.

Rites of transfer

In the last chapter we saw abjurations for those recounting a forced conversion to Catholicism. Issues of transfer also exist in this period. One of the earliest is the liturgy found in the 1700 Book of Common Prayer of the Church of Ireland, in which is added a service called 'A form for the receiving lapsed Protestants, or reconciling converted Papists to our Church'. It was believed that this was written by Anthony Dopping, Bishop of Meath, and it manifests the polemical approach of the day.[17] In England a 'Form for the Admitting Converted Roman Catholics to the Established Church' was produced in 1714 by Archbishop Tennison.[18] The context required rites of transfer.

Postscript

The mission consciousness of the Church of England and Anglicanism grew in the eighteenth and nineteenth century. Through evangelization Anglicans were required to perform adult baptism, and the catechumenate in a renewed form was developed in many places in order to foster and develop adult converts. This also resulted in the use of key festivals for baptism. While the desire for liturgy to be simple was strong in the eighteenth century, the minority interest was of making the ritual more complex and Eastern. Liturgical complexity was developed significantly in the nineteenth century by a Roman or medieval romantic liturgical movement. This, however, was linked to a strong mission commitment and thus variant forms of Anglicanism were planted around the world from Britain. To this should be added the work of American evangelists, who exported American liturgy and polity to the mission field. One particular aspect of their work was in the development of the idea and practice of the missionary bishop.

Changes in culture at home, including war, urbanization and a shift in society away from Christianity, led to a reconsideration of mission strategy, and this was combined with a vigorous liturgical renewal. This is considered in Chapter 6.

Notes

1 Church of England, 1662, 1968, *The Book of Common Prayer*, Cambridge: Cambridge University Press.

2 Phillip Tovey, 2014, *Anglican Confirmation: 1662–1820*, Farnham: Ashgate.

3 Alexander Nowell, 1570, 1853, *A Catechism Written in Latin*, trans. G. E. Corrie, Cambridge: Cambridge University Press; Robert Nelson, 1762, *A Companion for the Festivals and Fasts of the Church of England with Collects and Prayers for Each Solemnity*, London: T. Osborne.

4 Thomas Bray, 1703, *Catechetical Lectures on the Preliminary Questions and Answers of the Church-Catechism. Giving an Account of the Whole Doctrine of the Covenant of Grace*, London: printed by J. Brudenell for William Haws; Samuel Clarke, 1729, *An Exposition of the*

Church-Catechism. By Samuel Clarke, published from the Author's Manuscript, by John Clarke, London: printed by W. Botham, for James and John Knapton; Thomas Secker, 1790, *Lectures on the Catechism of the Church of England: With a Discourse on Confirmation*, London: printed for J. Rivington and Sons, St Paul's Churchyard, and B. White and Son, at Horace's Head, Fleet Street.

5 Tovey, *Anglican Confirmation*. Much of the eighteenth-century material can be found here in more detail.

6 John Wesley, 1784, *The Sunday Service of the Methodists in North America: With Other Occasional Services*, London.

7 Mohawk Book of Common Prayer, 1780. *The order for morning and evening prayer, and administration of the sacraments, and some other offices of the Church of England, together with a collection of prayers, and some sentences of the Holy Scriptures, necessary for knowledge and practice. Ne yakawea. Niyadewighniserage yondereanayendakhkwa orhoenkéne, neoni yogarask-ha oghseragwégouh . . . 3rd edn., formerly collected and translated into the Mohawk or Iroquois language, under the direction of the missionaries from the Venerable Society for the Propagation of the Gospel in Foreign Parts, to the Mohawk Indians. Rev. with corrections and additions by Daniel Claus.* Quebec: W. Brown, printer.

8 Stephen Neill, 1985, *A History of Christianity in India 1707–1858*, Cambridge: Cambridge University Press, pp. 216 ff.

9 See, S. Neill, *Christianity in India*, p. 216, n. p. 508.

10 Eugene Stock, 1899, *The History of the Church Missionary Society*, Vol. 3, London: Church Missionary Society, p. 564.

11 F. R. Graves, 1899, *Letter and Resolutions of the Conference of the Bishops of the Anglican Communion in China Hongkong and Corea held in Shanghai October 14th–20th 1899*, Shanghai: no publisher.

12 Anglican Church in Korea, 1905, *Office for the Admission of Catechumens*, Seoul Press: Hodge & Co.

13 The Annual Report of the Melanesian Mission for 1901, from *The Island Voyage and Report*, Auckland, 1902, pp. 1–12.

14 C. Lewis and G. E. Edwards, 1935, *South Africa: The Growth of the Church of the Province*, London: SPCK, p. 23.

15 H. P. Thompson, 1933, *Worship in Other Lands*, London: SPG.

16 Charles Wolhers, *The Book of Common Prayer, Occasional (Pastoral) Offices in Nsenga (1956)*, http://justus.anglican.org/resources/bcp/Zambia/nsenga.html (accessed 2014).

17 F. Procter and W. H. Frere, 1949, *A New History of the Book of Common Prayer*, London: Macmillan, p. 234.

18 'On the Form for Admitting Converted Roman Catholics to the Established Church' in *The Christian Examiner and Church of Ireland magazine*, Vol. 4, January to June 1827, pp. 260–4.

6

Home Mission: Developments in England

The Church of England had at last taken mission seriously and the Anglican Communion was developing. Empire continued for much of the twentieth century, but then came the era of political independence. Preceding and alongside that came the independence of Anglican Provinces and the development of the Anglican Communion. A number of factors in the twentieth century were a big influence on the Church of England. Some had a direct influence on liturgy and mission, others were more indirect – this chapter will concentrate on the most significant in relation to baptism and mission.

The 1928 failed prayer book

The Church of England came out of the First World War aware that many groups among the English population were alienated from the Church and from the Book of Common Prayer. Illusions had been shattered about the depth of Christian belief in the country, and although the notion of a Christian country was still strong in some sections of society, the chaplains from the front reported that this was very shallow in practice for many people.[1]

There had been a desire for Church reform of liturgy due to a number of factors. One was the development of ritualism and the changes that the ritualists made to the actual practice of the liturgy (even while the text of the prayer book was, as yet, unaltered). The Church authorities had recognized that taking the more extreme ritualists to court was not a successful strategy and merely created martyrs. There was a growing realization of the need to revise the Book of Common Prayer. This movement was also driven by further liturgical studies.

One part of the theological agenda was a debate started by Frederick Puller and Arthur Mason on the nature of confirmation. Mason had asserted:

> Baptism and confirmation can only be regarded, by those who value the teaching of antiquity, as forming together one sacrament.[2]

This of course comes from a particular reading that baptism and confirmation are two distinct things in patristic texts. It is a reading back using our lenses into what happened in the early Church. We must remember that if we asked Ambrose, Bishop of Milan from 374, 'What is confirmation?' he would not understand the question and might have well asked us the same question back! There was in his time one unified rite in which people were baptized, anointed, and received to communion, as we have seen above. Mason found in the fathers one sacrament in two parts and reapplied this to the present practice where the two parts are much divided by time. Mason's view was vigorously refuted by the high church priest in South Africa, Augustus Wirgman, at the end of the nineteenth century. However, it remained in the background and still influenced some people's thinking well into the twentieth century.[3]

In order to change the liturgy, the Church had to bring the revised Book of Common Prayer to parliament in order to make the liturgy speak to the new context of society. First, a new book was debated in the Church Assembly, where there was much discussion (possibly more outside the assembly than in), and in July 1927 the book was passed with large majorities in each of the houses. In December 1927 the Archbishop of Canterbury moved the Prayer Book Measure in the House of Lords for royal assent. The debate continued over three days and gained a clear majority. It then moved to the House of Commons where, after a long debate, it was narrowly rejected. The Church therefore decided to try a second time and made some changes to things that had been objectionable, particularly reservation. Thus, in 1928, the Church Assembly voted on the revised book, which once again got a majority, this time slightly slimmer. Debate raged in the country once again. In June 1928 the measure came back to the House of Commons and once again was defeated. A quick look at the figures showed that the Scottish and Welsh MPs had consistently voted against the book and most of the MPs from those constituencies were not Anglicans.[4]

This was a great shock to the Church; something that had been approved by the Church Assembly twice was turned down by parliament. It was clear that the Church of England needed an alternative way to develop its own liturgy, freed from the shackles of state interference. This was to come in 1964/5 with the Prayer Book (Alternative and other Services) Measure which enabled the Church to authorize by General Synod alternative liturgies to be available alongside the Book of Common Prayer.

There were two attempts to use parts of the 1928 prayer book. One was the *Churchpeople's Prayer Book and the Sacraments of the Church* which appeared in 1935 and was the work of the Bishop of Monmouth. The other was the very popular *Shorter Prayer Book* of 1947 which was widely used and incorporated 1928 material, including for confirmation. They also formed the basis for much of what was later published as *Alternative Services Series 1* – the first in the range of alternative services which followed the 1965 measure. Baptism and confirmation services often include many who have yet to come to faith and so there is a key missional opportunity in the service.

The 'Alternative Order of Public Baptism' provided by 1928 made the blessing of the water more prominent; beginning with a dialogue like the eucharistic prayer, it avoided the controversial language of 'regeneration' by using 'born-again' instead, and tightened up the duties of the godparents by asking them to commit themselves to their task. The 1928 alternative order of confirmation added verses from Acts 8 as part of the preface to the service to justify confirmation and rewrote the renewal of baptismal vows. The *Shorter Prayer Book* used the 1928 public baptism of infants, but for confirmation followed 1662 except for the alternative text from 1928 for the preface and for the renewal of baptismal vows. *Series 1* contained all the 1928 baptism provision, including referring to adult baptism as the baptism of those of 'riper years' even in 1967. Part of the aim of all this was to make the requirements of discipleship more clear.

The ecumenical movement

Seen as beginning at the world missionary conference of 1910, the ecumenical movement was a major influence in the twentieth century. Questioning the need to replicate the divisions of the Church in Europe and North America in missionary work around the world, and practically understanding the need for some division of territory among missionary societies, the movement developed by questioning the divisions of the Church and seeking its unity. The common understanding of baptism has been one of the key areas of work for the World Council of Churches, which grew out of this movement. 'One Lord, one faith, one baptism' (Eph. 4.5).

Perhaps most important in this ecumenical search is the document *Baptism, Eucharist and Ministry*.[5] This Faith and Order paper was produced by the World Council of Churches in 1982 and commented on by the participating churches. It generated a common language by which baptism was discussed and made clearer commonalities, differences and convergence. The document begins with the risen Christ sending his disciples into the world and commanding them to baptize. It sees five particular meanings of baptism:

1 A participation in Christ's death and resurrection
2 Conversion, pardoning and cleansing
3 The gift of the Holy Spirit
4 Incorporation into the body of Christ
5 The sign of the kingdom.

It sees baptism as both God's gift to us and our response in faith. It is the beginning of a lifelong growth in Christ. Differences about the place of children in relation to baptism were fully discussed, and the major differences acknowledged and articulated. Liturgically the document suggested that there were a number of elements that should be included in baptism rites: proclamation of Scripture, invocation of the Holy Spirit, renunciation of evil, profession of faith in Christ and the Holy Trinity, the use of water, a declaration of new identity as a child of God, and that members of the Church were called to witness to the gospel. It admitted that others would include the necessity of a sealing of the baptized with the gift of the Holy Spirit and participation in Holy Communion. The document is still worthy of study.

The ongoing work of the World Council of Churches in baptism has continued with the publication of two books of liturgical texts, *Baptism and Eucharist: Ecumenical Convergence in Celebration* and *Baptism Today*, and two further Faith and Order papers: *One Baptism: Towards Mutual Recognition* and *The Church: Towards a Common Vision*.[6] The outcome of this discussion has been the mutual recognition of baptism between many churches, and a welcome to the Lord's Table based on baptism rather than any particular denominational requirements. Clearly this is only a partial convergence between some denominations, and the ecumenical discussion needs to continue before recognizing baptism can be the basis for welcome to the table for all Christians. Christian disunity is a stumbling block to Christian witness.

While the World Council of Churches engages in multilateral discussions, there are also bilateral conversations. In relation to the Church of England, one of the most important is the Anglican–Baptist dialogue and the report *Conversations around the World 2000–2005*.[7] This saw initiation as a process, a journey in which there were a number of elements: teaching, profession of faith, baptism, membership of the Church, conversion and repentance. Viewing initiation in this way enabled the two churches to see that both had a journey with similar common elements, but not necessarily in the same order. There is however a tension between the notions of initiation as a journey and the completeness of the baptismal event.

The Lambeth Conference and Anglican documents

Beginning in 1867, the Lambeth Conference has met roughly every ten years as a gathering of Anglican bishops from around the world. While not a legislative body, it has often produced resolutions that have a strong impact on the Provinces of the Anglican Communion. In the post-war period a gradual change can be seen in the discussion of baptism and confirmation.

The 1948 conference was quite traditional in its resolutions. 'The conference considers that it is not desirable to change the present sequence of Baptism, Confirmation, and admission to Holy Communion.' This conference tried to strengthen traditional practice but suggested that baptism should more frequently be administered in regular church services, that no unbaptized person should be a godparent, that there should be proper preparation for confirmation, and that confirmation candidates should be encouraged to accept a rule of life. Perhaps the one new thing that Lambeth 1948 envisaged is the opportunity for an individual reaffirmation of baptismal vows and rededication.

The 1958 conference was in a completely different mood.[8] It recognized that 'no prayer book, not even that of 1662, can be kept unchanged for ever' and that we were entering a period of liturgical change. As such, the conference considered the services of the Church with suggestions for liturgical change. With regard to baptism it noted that there were a number of reports in various Provinces that were worthy of further consideration. It suggested that there needed to be a revised service of adult baptism and that this service should be related to confirmation and culminate in first communion. Twelve elements for a baptismal service were suggested:

1 Ministry of the word, teaching on baptism
2 Renunciation of the former way of life

3 Profession of faith in Christ with the reciting of the baptismal creed
4 Promises to hold fast to the Christian faith, obey God's commandments and witness to Christ
5 Blessing of the water
6 Baptism with water in the threefold name of God
7 Signing with the cross as a sign we have been bought with a price
8 Reception of the baptized person into the fellowship of the Church
9 Thanksgiving for having been sealed by the Holy Spirit
10 Prayer for growth in the Christian life
11 Exhortation to the congregation to support the candidate
12 Exhortation to the candidate to live their life in the power of the Spirit.

This provided the churches with an agenda for change and some pointers as to the direction in which to go. In particular it wanted to affirm the need for the provision of a service of adult baptism, confirmation and Holy Communion as one service and commended this to the whole Anglican Communion. While not explicitly expressing this in the context of mission, it is clear that the emphasis on the importance of adult baptism is part of a refocusing on mission.

The 1968 Lambeth Conference had less to say on baptism, save that Christians baptized in the name of the Trinity and communicant in their own Church should be welcomed to the Lord's table in Anglican churches. It also suggested that the confirmation rubric should not be read in such a way as to undermine this principle. Resolution 25 asked Provinces to explore the theology of baptism and confirmation and to experiment in this regard. This led to significant changes in New Zealand, the USA and Scotland and, as we shall see, a more ambivalent response in England.

The 1988 conference started with the mission of the church.[9] This affirmed the four marks of mission one of which was 'to teach, baptize and nurture new believers'. Having put baptism so central to mission, it then relegates liturgy to the end of the section report, seeing it as internal to the Church. It is a shame that such a narrow vision of liturgy and worship was held by the bishops. Nevertheless, later in the documents it included some very positive statements. 'Baptism by water is the scriptural statement of once for all initiation into Christ and into his body.' It notes that 'baptism should lead into communion' and that this had been strongly argued, and was being endorsed by some Provinces. This challenged the situation where many got baptized and confirmed but did not go on to receive communion.

The 1988 conference made further strong statements about baptism in its resolutions:

> All persons are made full disciples and equally members of the Body of Christ and the people or laos of God, by their baptism – Resolution III.22a.
>
> All the baptized share in the common priesthood of the Church – III.22b.

The 1988 conference made mission central, but failed to see the relationship between liturgy and mission.

Internationally, the work of the International Anglican Liturgical Consultation (IALC) has been important. These gatherings of liturgists from around the Communion have taken place since 1985. They do not have any binding authority on Provinces, but have been influential, especially in shaping the work of the provincial liturgical commissions (where they exist) and the revision of liturgical resources. The 1991 gathering of the IALC in Toronto (and the report it issued) was an important milestone in the Anglican discussion of initiation. This was particularly so because the liturgists, unlike the bishops, were keen to put baptism and mission together.[10] The report included seven recommendations on principles of initiation which are worth quoting in full.

1 The renewal of baptismal practice is an integral part of mission and evangelism. Liturgical texts must point beyond the life of the church to God's mission in the world.
2 Baptism is for people of all ages, both adults and infants. Baptism is administered after preparation and instruction of the

candidates, or where they are unable to answer for themselves, of their parent(s) or guardian(s).

3 Baptism is complete sacramental initiation and leads to participation in the eucharist. Confirmation and other rites of affirmation have a continuing pastoral role in the renewal of faith among the baptized but are in no way to be seen as a completion of baptism or as necessary for admission to communion.

4 The catechumenate is a model for preparation and formation for baptism. We recognize that its constituent liturgical rites may vary in different cultural contexts.

5 Whatever language is used in the rest of the baptismal rite, both the profession of faith and baptismal formula should continue to name God as Father, Son, and Holy Spirit.

6 Baptism once received is unrepeatable and any rites of renewal must avoid being misconstrued as rebaptism.

7 The pastoral rite of confirmation may be delegated by the Bishop to a presbyter.

This is a highly significant set of conclusions and was accompanied by a series of essays exploring different aspects of these principles. As the seven points are not binding, different Provinces have implemented different points. Within the Church of England it is possible to see catechumenal material, rites of renewal, and a mission focus as continuing the agenda encouraged by the above statement. Unfortunately these points never received a serious discussion either in General Synod or in the dioceses.

Internal Church of England debate

As well as discussion on the international level, there has been considerable discussion within the Church of England on both liturgy and mission. In terms of baptism and liturgy there seems to have been at least one paper to each quinqennium of the General Synod throughout its life – on average one every 18 months. In terms of mission there have been a whole series of documents including: *Towards the Conversion of England* (1945), *Finding*

Faith Today (1992), *Building Missionary Congregations* (1996) and *Mission-Shaped Church* (2004).

From a liturgical perspective two reports particularly stand out. One is *Christian Initiation: Birth and Growth in the Christian Society* (1971), otherwise called the Ely report. The other is *On the Way: Towards an Integrated Approach to Christian Initiation* (1995), which developed contextually some of the Toronto material from the IALC. Both of these reports will be further discussed in later chapters.

After the Second World War liturgical revision was suggested by an important report, *Baptism and Confirmation* (1958), which set some clear principles that have come to form the basis for much further liturgical revision. The report notes the inadequacy of working from a service for infants to a service for adults. It states quite clearly that 'in the new Testament adult baptism is the norm'. This is combined with the idea that the joint baptism and confirmation of adults with Holy Communion is the 'archetypal service'. Part of the argument was that confirmation arose after infants became the main candidates. The episcopal section of the united service of initiation was omitted at baptism and performed later in life. This of course assumes that there are parts reserved for the bishop only, which we have seen was not the only pattern, but the view gained ground because of its association with Rome. A united archetypal service has been the consistent position of all Church of England liturgical revision from *Series 2* to the *Alternative Service Book*. In *Common Worship* there is an alternative archetype. It is supplemented by provision for infant baptism and confirmation as stand-alone services. These liturgical discussions are alongside a growing awareness of adult baptism becoming more common.

The desire for reform

The post-war period has produced a whole series of discussions about different types of reform. These include discussions on the theological level, with particular points about baptismal theology and the theology of confirmation. They also include discussions focused on a mission level, about the pastoral application of the liturgy and policies for those who bring children for baptism but are otherwise unconnected with regular church life. There have been discussions too on a sociological level, particularly with relevance to the debate about whether England is a Christian country and what difference that might make. Alongside all this there has been a discussion of secularization and the keeping of statistics that showed that numbers of infant baptisms continued to decline. Indeed, the place of statistics in arguments has increased throughout the period. All of these need to be briefly looked at.

The changes of Vatican II produced optimism about possible reform within the Roman Catholic Church and beyond. Building on the same impetus for change, *Parish and People* sponsored an ecumenical conference on baptism, producing the book, *Crisis for Baptism* (1965).[11] This was willing to be radical, suggesting that adult baptism be the norm and the children of the uncommitted be admitted to a catechumenate. A similar book was developed a few years later: *Crisis for Confirmation* (1967).[12] Again the suggestion was that there was a need for reform, but there was little commonality as to what that should be. Part of the background to both these books, with their striking titles, is a discussion of indiscriminate baptism, and also indiscriminate confirmation. It would appear that some pastoral practice included little in terms of preparation. While all could agree that some preparation was necessary, not everyone was agreed as to what degree of preparation was required. Clifford Owen, in *Reforming Infant Baptism* (1990), classified parishes and their approaches in six different categories:

1 baptize all comers, with no questions asked;
2 baptize all, but with some preparation;
3 a 'hurdles' policy, requiring longer preparation;
4 a 'communicant status' requirement from one of the parents;
5 a rigorist approach, offering baptism for church members' children only; and
6 a policy offering baptism only to those who could answer for themselves.[13]

He defined 'indiscriminate' as including the first three levels and parts of the fourth. His definition is arguably much stricter than the canons of the Church of England.

At the beginning of this post-war period many Christians still considered that England was a Christian nation. Indeed that belief continued for quite a long time, despite statistical information to the contrary. There has always been a very slippery discussion as to what we envisage a Christian nation to be, and from time to time the question resurfaces. There are those who have argued for the importance of what is sometimes referred to as 'open baptism' for maintaining the notion of a Christian country. Perhaps one of the fullest exponents of this theory is R. R. Osborn in *Forbid Them Not* (1972).[14] Here a policy of baptizing all comers with some Christian nurture is seen to support a Christian nation. If Callum Brown is correct, during the sixties the country itself turned away from this, such that its self-identification became not Christian but either secular or multicultural.[15] It is also important to notice an ecclesiological change in thinking alongside societal change. Osborn envisaged a Christian country in which the Church, the state, and general baptism formed three parts of a triangle. It classically rests very much on mixed field model of the Church; one that contains both wheat and tares growing together. It may also rest less on a conversionist view of salvation and more on an Augustinian concept of predestination, or a more modern universalistic theology. There has been a growing change in ecclesiology such that a gathered church model is now much more dominant; Christ against culture rather than Christ in culture. It would be hard now to find anyone supporting general baptism without any form of preparation, but it is also hard to find a thought-through understanding about the place of the Church and its baptismal policy within a multicultural nation.

The most controversial theological issue around initiation came from the work of Gregory Dix. In 1946 he gave a lecture in Oxford on the theology of confirmation in relation to baptism.[16] Dix supported the view of Mason, which he erroneously said had never been refuted, and he also reacted to the report *Confirmation Today* (1944), which he felt had downplayed confirmation, perhaps for ecumenical reasons, as could be seen if put alongside the South India reunion proposals. He argued for a two-part initiation – baptism and confirmation; so one is initially baptized into Christ's death and resurrection, followed separately by a sealing with the Spirit at confirmation. This was a highly contentious re-reading of the patristic material. Geoffrey Lampe refuted Dix in his book, *The Seal of the Spirit* (1951).[17] He carefully looked at the patristic evidence and was unable to separate the Spirit from the water bath. He also continued a more direct attack on Dix's theory in various articles. Biblically the argument was finally scuppered by James Dunn in *Baptism in the Holy Spirit* (1970).[18] While Dunn was primarily interested in Pentecostal claims, at the same time he looked at Anglo-Catholic interpretations and found them wanting in Scripture. Understanding our theology influences our pastoral and missional practice.

A variety of groupings within the Church of England participated in the ongoing debate. In an earlier period, the Parish and People movement had organized some conferences and within that some more liberal voices were able to be heard. Eric James, in the 1965 conference on baptism, said that he thought we had not grasped the meaning of baptism, were speaking our own internal language, and what was needed was not a tidy policy but living the baptismal life. He reminded people of the teaching of F. D. Maurice, that baptism proclaims what a child is, that Christ's work is completed and we are already his children.[19] It is not that in baptism we become his children, but that in baptism we are proclaiming that we are already his children. This he found more satisfactory in terms of pastoral experience. The alternative was to increasingly fence the font, depending upon your definition of a Christian.

Throughout the period the Alcuin Club continued to publish a whole series of books on baptism and confirmation. Some of these were of historical importance, including not least, J. D. C. Fisher's, *Christian Initiation: Baptism in the Medieval West* (1965).[20] This book contained the main exposition of the disintegration of the patristic rite and the basis for the argument of a united 'archetypal service'. There were books that discussed the various theological positions being taken,[21] and books of collections of baptismal texts.[22] All of this helped to inform debate. Coming along slightly later and from an evangelical perspective, Grove Books have produced an influential series of publications in the initiation area. Picking up on Lampe and the Ely report, E. C. Whitaker published the first Grove Liturgical Study, *Sacramental Initiation Complete in Baptism* (1975).[23] The title makes clear the thesis of the book and this was a scholarly discussion of biblical and patristic evidence. Of particular significance has been a series of books by Colin Buchanan, supporting infant baptism, arguing for its reform, resisting re-baptism, and rejecting two-stage theories of initiation.[24] This has not only been a theoretical discussion but has also been a movement for practical change, championed by The Movement for the Reform of Infant Baptism (known more recently as Baptism Integrity) which was formed in 1987. This led to much discussion of 'open' and 'closed' baptismal policies of individual parishes and was a big influence on practical mission in parishes.[25]

Within this milieu the Liturgical Commission had to develop new baptismal rites. These came with *Series 2* (1968), *Series 3* (1979) and the *Alternative Service Book* (1980). With no consensus on the direction of reform, the writing of the liturgies was a difficult task. *Series 3* was the first to use modern language. This in and of itself produced another wave of debate and discussion in that some thought prayer should be in traditional language as a sign of reverence, others wanted modern English to enhance discipleship and mission. Others were unhappy with the content of the language, for example, in the peace, commenting that the strong expression of 'we are the body of Christ' might lead to an inward looking Church with a gathered mentality, which might then change baptismal approaches.[26] Others disliked the way the *Series 2* infant baptism service was unclear about the articulation of faith. It appeared that the parents were asked if they believed, but the candidate was not required to say anything at all. This was changed by the phrase which came in in *Series 3* (and was retained in *The Alternative Service Book, 1980*) 'you must answer for yourselves and for this child'. The option for anointing with oil was also quietly introduced in baptism and confirmation. While in the 1950s its value had been questioned in a modern society, it was allowed as an option within *Series 3* as an expression of 'breadth' within the Church of England.

Liturgical revision happened not only in this country, and the influence of the Episcopal Church in the United States of America should also be mentioned. Their discussion of the potential revision of baptism and confirmation began with *Prayer Book Studies 1* in 1950. This, while cautious of extreme Dixian views, still argued for an important place for confirmation as a Spirit-endowing ritual. By *Prayer Book Studies 26* (1973) a completely different view had been taken.[27] Baptism was now seen as complete sacramental initiation, and confirmation was in a separate section of the book as a pastoral rite of reaffirmation of vows. This change did not reflect a takeover of the Episcopal Church by evangelicals, but the conversion of Anglican-Catholics in that Church to baptism completing sacramental initiation. As the American material is relatively easy to access (and Americans have played a big part in the IALC meetings), the discussions over the pond have continued to have influence in England.

Postscript

As can be seen, the discussion on baptism and rites of initiation has continued on a variety of levels, ecumenical, theological, liturgical and missional. The debate has been fierce and as yet in England has not come to final conclusions. Other Provinces in the Anglican Communion have taken reform in directions that enshrine the view that sacramental initiation is complete in baptism. The baptismal debates about theology and liturgy are debates about the Church's self-understanding in a new context and about the missional response in that context.

Notes

1 See, F. B. MacNutt, 1917, *The Church in the Furnace*, London: Macmillan.

2 Arthur Mason, 1891, *The Relation of Confirmation to Baptism, as Taught in Holy Scripture and the Fathers*, London: Longmans, p. 1. See also, F. W. Puller, 1880, *What Is the Distinctive Grace of Confirmation?* Cambridge: Rivingtons.

3 A. Wirgman, 1897, *The Doctrine of Confirmation*, London: Longmans.

4 Donald Gray, 2005, *The 1927–28 Prayer Book Crisis 1*, Joint Liturgical Studies 60, Norwich: SCM-Canterbury Press; Donald Gray, 2006, *The 1927–28 Prayer Book Crisis 2*, Joint Liturgical Study 61, Norwich: SCM-Canterbury Press.

5 World Council of Churches, 1982, *Baptism, Eucharist and Ministry*, Faith and Order Paper 111, Geneva: World Council of Churches; World Council of Churches, 2013, *The Church: Towards a Common Vision*, Faith and Order Paper 214, Geneva: World Council of Churches.

6 M. Thurian and G. Wainwright, 1983, *Baptism and Eucharist: Ecumenical Convergence in Celebration*, Geneva: World Council of Churches; Thomas Best, 2008, *Baptism Today: Understanding, Practice, Ecumenical Implications*, Collegeville: Liturgical Press; World Council of Churches, 2011, *One Baptism: Towards Mutual Recognition: A Study Text*, Faith and Order Paper 210, Geneva: World Council of Churches; World Council of Churches, 2013, *The Church: Towards a Common Vision,* Faith and Order Paper 214, Geneva: World Council of Churches.

7 Anglican Communion Office and Baptist World Alliance, 2005, *Conversations around the World 2000–2005: The Report of the International Conversations between the Anglican Communion and the Baptist World Alliance*, London: Anglican Communion Office.

8 Lambeth Conference, 1958, *The Lambeth Conference 1958: The Encyclical Letter from the Bishops Together with the Resolutions and Reports*, London: SPCK.

9 Lambeth Conference, 1988, *The Truth Shall Make You Free: The Lambeth Conference 1988: The Reports, Resolutions & Pastoral Letters from the Bishops,* London: Church House Publishing.

10 D. R. Holeton (ed.), 1993, *Growing in Newness of Life: Christian Initiation in Anglicanism Today: Papers from the Fourth International Anglican Liturgical Consultation, Toronto, 1991,* Toronto: Anglican Book Centre.

11 B. S. Moss, 1965, *Crisis for Baptism: The Report of the 1965 Ecumenical Conference Sponsored by the Parish and People Movement,* London: SCM Press.

12 M. C. Perry (ed.), 1967, *Crisis for Confirmation*, London: SCM Press.

13 Clifford Owen, (ed.), 1990, *Reforming Infant Baptism*, London: Hodder & Stoughton.

14 R. R. Osborn, 1972, *Forbid Them Not: The Importance and the History of General Baptism,* London: SPCK. See also M. Dalby, 1989, *Open Baptism*, London: SPCK; and D. Gray, 'Baptizing the Nation', in D. R. Holeton, 1993, *Growing in Newness of Life*, Toronto: Anglican Book Centre, pp. 197–9.

15 Callum Brown, 2009, *The Death of Christian Britain,* London: Routledge.

16 G. Dix, 1946, *The Theology of Confirmation in Relation to Baptism*, London: Dacre Press.

17 G. W. H. Lampe, 1967, *The Seal of the Spirit: A Study in the Doctrine of Baptism and Confirmation in the New Testament and the Fathers*, 2nd edn, London: SPCK.

18 James Dunn, 1970, *Baptism in the Holy Spirit: A Re-Examination of the New Testament Teaching on the Gift of the Spirit in Relation to Pentecostalism Today*, Naperville: A. R. Allenson.

19 A. R. Vidler, 1966, *F.D. Maurice and Company*. London: SCM Press.

20 J. D. C. Fisher, 1965, *Christian Initiation: Baptism in the Medieval West*, Alcuin Club Collection 47, London: SPCK.

21 J. D. C. Fisher, 1978, *Confirmation Then and Now,* Alcuin Club Collection 60, London: SPCK.

22 E. C. Whitaker, 1960, *Documents of the Baptismal Liturgy,* London: SPCK.

23 E. C. Whitaker, 1975, *Sacramental Initiation Complete in Baptism*, Grove Liturgical Study 1, Bramcote: Grove Books.

24 C. O. Buchanan, 1973, 1978, *A Case for Infant Baptism,* Grove Worship Series 20, Bramcote: Grove Books; C. O. Buchanan, 1972, *Baptismal Discipline,* Grove Worship Series 3, Bramcote: Grove Books; C. O. Buchanan, 1978, *One Baptism Once,* Grove Worship Series 61, Bramcote: Grove Books; C. O. Buchanan, 1986, *Anglican Confirmation,* Grove Liturgical Study No. 48, Bramcote: Grove Books; C. O. Buchanan, 1993, *The Renewal of Baptismal Vows,* Grove Worship Series 124, Bramcote: Grove Books; C. O. Buchanan, 1993, *Infant Baptism and the Gospel,* London: Darton, Longman and Todd.

25 M. Dalby, 1989, *Open Baptism,* London: SPCK.

26 David Cockerell, 1980, 'The Language of Initiation: A Critique of Series 3 Baptism' in *Modern Churchman* 23, No. 1: 21–9.

27 Ruth Meyers, 1997, *Continuing the Reformation: Re-Visioning Baptism in the Episcopal Church*, New York: Church Publishing.

7

Ely and Onwards: the Death of Christian Society

As we have seen, there was a whole series of official Church of England reports in the post-war period including *Confirmation Today* (1944) and *Baptism and Confirmation Today* (1954).[1] However, their recommendations were largely shelved or ignored, save perhaps for the unified rite theory, which argued for the priority of adult baptism in which the adult candidate would be baptized, confirmed and receive first communion in one ceremony. The sixties saw big changes in society and an increasing division between the Church and a nation no longer necessarily self-consciously Christian. This led to much discussion in the Church about baptism, and those coming for baptism or, more significantly, bringing their children for baptism. In the need to bridge the gulf between the Church and society were the beginnings of the Family Service movement, which saw many churches take an approach to Sunday worship that moved beyond matins or Holy Communion to something more informal, teaching-focused and child-friendly. The Church was also aware of big changes in religious education and the impact of the mission of the Church through its schools. In the light of this the Church of England asked for a major report bringing together these aspects of Christian initiation and holistic mission through education. The result was *Christian Initiation: Birth and Growth in a Christian Society* (1971), also called the Ely report.[2] This report was of major importance for approaches to baptism and mission, and one where the Church of England was called to vote on issues of major principle. The aftermath of this report and the discussion that followed it still continues to rumble on today. Thus it is important to look at the report and its recommendations.

The Ely report, 1971

In reviewing previous reports, Ely noted a certain move from radicalism to a more conservative position in the later reports. It suggested that timidity and uncertainty had contributed to current divergence, and commented that the only concrete thing to come out of the reports was a revision of the catechism, as carried out in 1962. It noted that the sixties produced a major change in society and that there was a larger gap between the Church and society with the development of Marxism, scientific humanism, and non-theist philosophy and psychology. It also noted that the Church had too readily identified with middle-class morality. Changes in approaches to authority had left an anti-authoritarian attitude, often developing at the same age that people would traditionally have gone for confirmation. John Robinson's book, *Honest to God* had stirred up much thinking about theology, both within the Church and beyond it, and there had been rapid changes in educational theory. All of these were seen as the social background to the report. The report made 16 recommendations, in seven different areas. It is still worth looking at the original report, but not all of its recommendations are of lasting significance.

The recommendations include that 'the church should make explicit its recognition of baptism as the full and complete rite of Christian initiation'. This is perhaps the main theological position, the principle on which the rest of the report is built. As a corollary of this the report thinks that baptism should take place in the main service, that secondary symbols should be encouraged where desired, and that infant baptism be properly administered to parents who express their 'sincere desire' for baptism.

The report recommended a service of thanksgiving for the birth of the child provided it not be regarded as a substitute for baptism. It was recommended that there be provision made at all levels of the Christian life for training and for training trainers in Christian nurture and development, a theme recently returned to in Synod.

The report wished to allow parish priests to admit persons to communion on the basis of baptism only. This would require preparation, and the report preferred that first communion be led by the bishop.

That recommendation raised the further question as to the nature of confirmation. This was seen as a service of commitment and commissioning for those in adult life. The report saw the possibility of the laying on of hands being done by the bishop or a priest appointed by the bishop.

For those baptized as adults, as a fruit of mission, the report considered that confirmation was unnecessary as all the commitments would have been made in the rite of adult baptism; this is the primary point of public commitment. This differs from those who are baptized as infants who need to make a public commitment for their baptismal response. This is done at confirmation. The report however hoped that for adults first communion would be administered by the bishop, as they wished the bishop to continue a role in mission and entry into the Church.

Finally, ecumenical considerations were taken into account, and it was suggested that confirmation should not be used as a rite for membership of the Church of England for people from other churches. People transferring should be admitted to communion after preparation if they had been validly baptized.

This was a radical set of proposals and started from a principled theological position that baptism is the full rite of initiation. In some ways it did not drive this as far as it could go, with admission to first communion being seen as a separate service in many cases in the recommendations, rather than integral to baptism. However it set out for Britain the position that was to be taken in other Provinces, for example, America, Canada and New Zealand. The aftermath of the report, however, was not as clear-cut as the report itself. This now needs to be examined.

Ely in the synodical process

The Church was now confronted with having to respond to the report, and work out a process for doing this. One response was to ask for a summary of the document and this was produced in

Christian Initiation: A Working Paper (Cornwell, 1973).[3] This was an unfortunate move as, while the paper has its own merits, in that it carefully discussed all the recommendations and debated them, it introduced further possible approaches, and developed further the criticisms of the Ely report. One concrete aspect of this is to discuss more clearly baptism and chrismation as full initiation.

The Synod then introduced a further paper, *Christian Initiation – A Discussion Paper*.[4] This recommended a series of background reading, the Ely report, the Doctrine Commission report on *Baptism, Thanksgiving and Blessing*, Cornwell's 'Working Paper' and its own report, and referred three areas to the dioceses to be voted on, first in the area of infant baptism, second in the area of services of thanksgiving and blessing, and third in the area of baptismal practice. This was not particularly well handled as voting showed that people were fairly muddled as to what they were being asked to do. Nevertheless they were not asked to vote on the key recommendation of principle that baptism was the full and complete rite of Christian initiation.

The dioceses voted in favour of the practice of infant baptism, but were not asked if this was full sacramental initiation in theory. However for the motion that there should be alternative provision (compared to the prayer book pattern of infant baptism, confirmation, communion) based on the idea of full sacramental initiation in baptism the dioceses narrowly voted in favour. The motion on allowing admission to communion by the priest, which one might think you would vote in favour of if you voted in favour of the alternative provision, was rejected by the diocesan synods. The motion which approved baptismal anointing followed by Holy Communion was widely rejected with only a small minority in favour.[5] This was a muddled response, as the questions had not really grown out of the Ely commission report. General Synod in 1976 rejected the proposition for an alternative initiation provision, baptism (as full initiation), first communion and confirmation.[6] This seemed to be an end to the Ely report.

However, this was not to be. The National Evangelical Anglican Congress in 1977 asked that Synod look again at the Ely report, affirmed that baptism is complete sacramental initiation into Christ and his body, wanted to see the separation of confirmation from admission to communion, and the abolition of the requirement of confirmation for those transferring from another church. Whatever had happened in General Synod, the issues did not lie down and were not decisively finished; the Church had to return to the issues Ely had raised.

The one positive upshot of the Ely process was considerable support for a rite of thanksgiving. It is probable, within a confused situation, that a conservative position basically upholding a prayer book process was the one that prevailed, but there was clearly also a large support for the Ely position, and some people had already gone ahead in admitting people to communion who were baptized (mostly children). This had particularly happened in the dioceses of Southwark and Manchester. Ely had opened a door, one that would prove impossible to shut. Indeed the lack of a clear decision on principle, led to a fragmentation of positions within the Church of England, and explains both the pastoral confusion and variety of opinions within the Church today. This needs some further exploration.

Models of initiation post Ely

I want to suggest that there are at least five different approaches to Christian initiation that developed in the post-Ely context.

The first is an approach that is taken by those who support the general position on initiation taken by the prayer book. This supports infant baptism, with some preparation, and then confirmation at a later age before admission to communion. Adults may also be baptized but still need to be confirmed. While this is a venerable position in the Church of England, it is also the position that has been gradually crumbling and led to all the other discussion and positions taken. It may still continue in some places in the country but in others has almost completely collapsed as churches have taken other routes. It also does not solve the question of confirmation. While it may well be a pastoral rite needed by those who have been baptized as infants, there has never developed a credible rationale for confirmation of those baptized as adults.

The second position is those who broadly take an Ely approach, which has continued to develop until today. This argues that baptism is full initiation, and that it should be possible to admit to communion all the baptized. The post-Ely debate was one of continuing support for this position, eventually leading to the Church having to admit that there were two possible approaches to admission to communion, even if only grudgingly allowing the admission before confirmation as an alternative approach.[7] Year after year the supporters of this approach have chipped away and gained success in doing so. Gradually there are parishes in every diocese that have taken up this approach. This has been bolstered somewhat by an inclusiveness argument, which instinctively wants to include children, which while a fine value should not be detached from the baptismal question. There is also some solid research to show that from a mission perspective this approach is more effective in supporting young people in faith than the traditional approach.[8]

The third approach is to broadly reject infant baptism.[9] Some people 'fenced the font' so tightly in their preparation requirements that infant baptisms began to wane in the parish completely. Some used the rite of thanksgiving for the birth of a child (or the more recent *Common Worship* 'Thanksgiving for the Gift of a Child') as a required preparatory service to baptism. For some using it this way the hope was this would be sufficient for people so that they would not come back for baptism and 'make promises that they have no intention of fulfilling'. This was not the original intention of this service of thanksgiving, and it was clearly stated that it was not a substitute for baptism; however, some in practice have used it in this way.

The fourth approach was to try to hold on to the remnants of a Dix theology, that baptism confers forgiveness and confirmation the Holy Spirit. While this has been academically discredited there have been continued attempts to resurrect the theory, and often to confuse it with a traditional prayer book approach, claiming it therefore as the Anglican norm, rather than an aberration. The recent report of the Faith and Order Commission (FAOC), *The Journey of Christian Initiation* (2011) seemed to try to resurrect this view based upon a dislike of the Ely position, a worry about Anglican–Baptist dialogue, and an attempt to reassert confirmation.[10] It has been refuted in detail by Colin Buchanan in a Grove Book, but shows how resistant some in the Church still are to the positions set out in the Ely report.[11]

A fifth approach, not perhaps ever explicitly stated, but hinted at by Peter Cornwell, supports a more Orthodox approach. This sees baptism and anointing as sufficient to be full initiation. As the possibilities of anointing gradually developed, particularly with chrismation after baptism being allowed in *Common Worship*, so some are able to view baptism and chrismation as full initiation and sufficient for receiving communion. This appears to be one of the positions approved by Cornwell and J. D. C. Fisher in his *The Fullness of Christian Initiation* and has a small minority of supporters in the dioceses.[12] It also seems to be the view of the Roman Catholic scholar Paul de Clercke, reflecting a similar discussion in Roman Catholicism.[13]

The *Alternative Service Book*

Decades of liturgical revision culminated in the *Alternative Service Book* (1980). This built on previous booklets, *Series 2* which began modern liturgical revision, and *Series 3* which used modern English for the first time. The Church was now able to write its own alternative services to the Book of Common Prayer, which remains as the normative service book of the Church of England. In pastoral practice the *Alternative Service Book* baptism service virtually completely replaced the provision in the BCP. Because there had been numerous experimental booklets over many years, and thus much discussion about appropriate liturgical forms, there was a high consensus around the services in the ASB. The Church of England had its first complete book that was the fruit of the liturgical movement; the aim was missional, to speak in a new language to the people.

Seventy pages of the book were devoted to initiation services. The first two services were thanksgiving for the birth of the child and thanksgiving after adoption. These were, in part, alternative to the churching of women. As such one is left wondering whether they were in the wrong section of the book and should have sat separately with other pastoral rites. The first note explains that the minister is supposed to say that this is not baptism and one of the prayers in the service asks God to direct the child that in due time they may be received by baptism into the Church. However, the pastoral practice of some parishes was to require that everyone have a thanksgiving before baptism. It is perhaps unfortunate that the thanksgiving service could have been made more like a service of introduction to the catechumenate. It then could have been used in a mission strategy of teaching and preaching with some commitment to families. The question of how to make requests for infant baptism foster mission and the discipleship that needs to be developed with it goes alongside the liturgical development.

The first service in the initiation section of the ASB was the archetypal service of 'Baptism, Confirmation and Holy Communion'; all other services were then derivatives from this. This is the strategy that the Church of England committed itself to in the 1958 report, *Baptism and Confirmation*, and has consistently followed since then. With regard to infants, the theological position taken was that of Christian family baptism (based on the household baptisms in the New Testament) where parents are assumed to be practising Christians. The service allowed the renewal of baptismal vows to be included at the bishop's discretion.

The ministry of the word gave a selection of readings with themes of baptism and the Spirit. The decision was three short questions including a renunciation of evil but not of the devil (following the tradition from *Series 2*). The questions were directed to the parents and godparents and made clear that they must answer both for themselves and for these children. This was in response to criticism of *Series 2* where it appeared that the parents and godparents were asked the questions, but not actually the child themselves. The prayer book tradition was that the child was answering through the godparents; here in the ASB the godparents renew their own baptismal vows while they are also answering for the child.

The decision was immediately followed by the signing with the cross. This was brought forward from after baptism to undermine the idea that baptism was about making the sign of the cross with a wet finger. The prayer of protection after the signing was a deliberate echo of catechumenal rites. A note allowed the signing of the cross to be performed with oil, which would be the oil of catechumens.

The prayer over the water occurred next, partially to allow profession of faith to be immediately followed by the baptism. In the prayer there was a functional blessing of the water; 'bless this water that your servants who are washed in it may be made one with Christ'. While there were no rubrics to touch the water at this point, many in practice made the sign of the cross in the water. Some objected to the blessing of an inanimate object, but this was no different from the blessing of the water in the Book of Common Prayer.

The declaration of faith came in three questions of Trinitarian form, echoing Hippolytus, an early account of baptismal practice. As in the decision, questions are 'for yourself and for these children'. They are followed by a Trinitarian acclamation by the congregation. Unfortunately the ASB came out before inclusive language became the norm in British English, and thus the second question which talks of Jesus redeeming 'mankind' was later to be reworked. Thus a number of alternatives were developed.[14] The administration of baptism was done in traditional Western form allowing either a single or triple pouring.

Post-baptismal ceremonies include the giving of a lighted candle to either the person baptized or a godparent and then confirmation follows. Here the prayer for the gift of the Spirit is said over the candidates with outstretched hands of the bishop, but the confirmation itself is with a single hand upon the candidate. The words 'Confirm, O Lord your servant with your Holy Spirit', are used at the laying on of the hand and imply a strengthening with the Holy Spirit, but leave open the exact nature of this strengthening. The prayer 'Defend O Lord' is the confirmation prayer in the Book of Common Prayer but here becomes a congregational petition for the candidates. The bishop then welcomes the candidates and a rubric allows the renewal of baptismal vows. This gives the bishop a key role in baptismal rites and expression of their leadership of mission in the diocese.

All the other services in the ASB are derivatives of this main rite to allow baptism and mission to work contextually in parishes. The baptism of children adds an introduction, but avoids using the 'let the children come unto me' passage (Mark 10.13–16). There had been criticism of the prayer book for using this as it is not clearly a baptismal passage. The stand-alone confirmation service adds the renewal of baptismal vows to the confirmation service, otherwise it is the same as the archetypal rite. Finally there is provision for conditional baptism and emergency baptism. The latter says that parents should be assured that ultimate salvation for a child that has died does not depend upon baptism. This was a denial of the Augustinian tradition, which had so shaped the Western Church.

Alongside the ASB was the growing popularity of family services. One reason these began was as a bridge for baptism families, to help them make the transition to regular worship in the Church. Kenneth Stevenson in 1981, the year after the ASB was produced, began to discuss these services including their mission element.[15] This was not to bear fruit until the report *Patterns for Worship* (1989) was published.[16] Although at that point the report was still just a General Synod paper (and published in that format), it sold like hot cakes and was used widely in the Church. The official version came in the booklet, *A Service of a Word*, in 1994 and in the published version of *Patterns for Worship* in 1995.[17] Thus baptism as it was presented in the ASB needed to be put in the context of wider liturgical provision of a missional nature.

Children and communion

The issue of admitting all the baptized to communion without requiring prerequisites (for example, confirmation) continued to be argued throughout the Church. Daniel Young in 1983 spoke in favour for evangelicals in *Welcoming Children to Communion*.[18] In

1985 an important report was produced for General Synod, *Communion before Confirmation?* often called the Knaresborough report.[19] This reaffirmed that baptism is a complete sacrament of initiation and that confirmation is not a prerequisite for admission to communion. It proposed a new canon which would allow the incumbent and PCC to vote for the parish to admit children to communion. Unfortunately this canon has never been produced. The Board of Education report *Children in the Way* (1988) encouraged a positive rethinking of the place of children in the church.[20] The British Council of Churches produced a report *Children and Holy Communion* in 1989; the issue was wider than the Church of England.[21] People were increasingly aware that other parts of the Anglican Communion had changed their practice, and parishes where Scots, Americans or New Zealanders had moved in might well discover families with children already receiving communion.

The progress of children and communion met a milestone in 1997 when the House of Bishops published guidelines on the admission of baptized persons to communion before confirmation. This was encouraged by a survey by Culham College Institute *Communion before Confirmation* (1993).[22] One of the few serious pieces of research on children and communion, it reported that in parishes where children were admitted to communion before confirmation there was a stronger sense of belonging, that children felt more a part of the church, and that children seemed to remain a part of the church longer. Confirmation appeared to be more of an adult commitment.

A series of questionnaires showed how many parishes were taking advantage of the guidelines and changing to the alternative practice:

Table 6 Parishes admitting children to communion before confirmation

Year	Number of parishes
2001	1,064
2002	1,226
2004	1,539
2005	1,650

Thus far there has been a growing movement of admitting children to communion. Ultimately one liturgical development of this was *Additional Eucharistic Prayers* (2012) which included directions on celebrating the Eucharist with children and two Eucharistic prayers suitable for when children are present.[23]

The 1997 guidelines were replaced in 2006 by regulations. Many people in the debate look forward to this being not a permissive activity in parishes, but one that is recognized as the standard or normative approach of the Church of England.[24] This probably will not come without a canon.

Baptismal policy

The concerns of some in the Church of England over what they considered to be 'indiscriminate' infant baptism led to considerable debate over baptismal policy. A key voice in this debate was Colin Buchanan, who approached the issue in a particular way, over a number of books and booklets, beginning with *Baptismal Discipline* (1972) which gives a case study of a baptismal policy in London.[25] In *A Case for Infant Baptism* (1973, 2009) Buchanan sets out a 'cumulative case' for infant baptism based on an examination of biblical texts showing the possibility of the baptism of children of believing families, expressed in the wording in the ASB.[26] Buchanan rejects the more traditional covenant theology based on Calvin's work. The debate was continued by the Movement for the Reform of Infant Baptism, now known as Baptismal Integrity.[27]

In 1989 Mark Dalby responded to Colin Buchanan with the book *Open Baptism*.[28] He particularly criticizes the limiting of Christian influence to the parents only, noting in Russia the importance of grandparents, and the actual difficulty in practice of distinguishing between the believer and the unbeliever. Is this limited to those who come every Sunday, to those who come monthly, or to those who come to the Carol service, Mothering Sunday and Remembrance Day? Dalby points to the Ely report's 'sincere desire' as the qualification for the parents. Dalby states that a church which baptizes widely will never have clearly defined boundaries. He might have developed this statement further to question the underlying ecclesiology of the different positions. Those with more rigorous baptismal policies may have much more of a gathered church approach, whereas those with open baptismal policies may have a more Augustinian approach, of the true Church being more hidden and the visible Church being a mixture of wheat and tares.

The setting of baptismal policy, with a debate between 'open' and 'strict' approaches, became a major exercise in many parishes. The focus often seemed to be on the integrity of the sacrament and a particular mission approach that made challenge an early part of the approach. Leslie Francis showed that while it was possible to have strict policies in urban areas, in rural areas this was a completely disastrous approach for church.[29] As dioceses and parishes are looking at mission action plans, so baptismal policy needs to be subsumed into this approach to mission. Baptism is the fruit of mission and a call to mission, but we need to look at our baptismal practice to see how it enhances mission.

Baptismal reordering

A less controversial area has been the development of the architecture of baptism. Increasingly Church of England churches have baptismal tanks designed for adult immersion alongside the traditional font. This was noted by the House of Bishops in a paper 'Baptism and Fonts' (1992).[30] The paper observed the increasing use of various types of pools to allow the candidate to be submerged. This is in part a response to the increasing number of adult candidates for baptism. While temporary pools are put up in some places, others have built baptism tanks or pools, often under the ground and covered when not in use.

The bishops wished to assert the principle of a single font in the church. However, they provided examples where there is an integration of design such that different modes of baptism may be able to proceed from one combined font and baptistery, recognizing both adult and infant baptism as equal responses to the gospel. They commented that 'Church buildings have a proclamatory life of their own apart from the confines of public worship.' This is a good point. Baptisteries that are under the platform in the church, and where the old font is now used as a flower display, seem to suggest that baptism is either unimportant or not a part of the ongoing life of the church. Baptisteries at the door suggest that entry to the church is through baptism. The redesign of baptismal space within a church is an important aspect of the architectural renewal of church buildings.[31]

Postscript

The Ely report set out the issue of principle that baptism is complete sacramental initiation. However, the Church of England never really grasped the nettle and thus runs a mixed economy of a traditional pattern alongside this alternative approach. The relationship of mission and baptism can be seen in liturgical texts and their renewal to enhance mission. The mission of the Church is even in the reordering of baptismal areas. The failure of the Ely process has left the Church with an ongoing debate about admission to communion, the place of confirmation and the theology of baptism in a mission context.

Notes

1 Joint Committee on Confirmation, 1944, *Confirmation to-day: Being the schedule attached to the interim reports of the Joint Committee on Confirmation, setting forth certain major issues before the church, as presented to the Convocations of Canterbury and York in October, 1944*, London: Press and Publications Board of the Church Assembly; Convocations of Canterbury and York, 1955, *Baptism and Confirmation to-day: Being the schedule attached to the final reports of the Joint Committees on Baptism, Confirmation, and Holy Communion, as presented to the Convocations of Canterbury and York in October, 1954*, London: SPCK.

2 Commission on Christian Initiation, 1971, *Christian Initiation: Birth and Growth in the Christian Society*, GS 30, London: Church Information Office.

3 R. P. Cornwell, 1973, *Christian Initiation: A Working Paper*, GS 184, London: Church Information Office.

4 General Synod, 1974, *Christian Initiation: A Discussion Paper*, London: Church Information Office.

5 General Synod, 1975, *Christian Initiation: Results of the Reference to the Diocesan Synods 1974–75*, GS 291a, London.

6 C. Buchanan, 1976, 'Initiation – No New Alternative Pattern', in *News of Liturgy*, 19, pp. 1–2.

7 M. A. Reardon, 1991, *Christian Initiation: A policy for the Church of England: a discussion paper*, GS Misc 635, London: Church House Publishing: K. Stevenson and D. Stancliffe, 1991, *Christian Initiation and its Relation to some Pastoral Offices: A paper prepared on behalf of the Liturgical Commission*, GS Misc 366, London: General Synod of the Church of England.

8 B. Kay, J. Greenough and J. D. Gay, 1993, *Communion before Confirmation: A Report on the Survey Conducted by Culham College Institute*, Abingdon: Culham College Institute.

9 See Alan Write in Clifford, Owen (ed.), 1990, *Reforming Infant Baptism*, London: Hodder & Stoughton.

10 Paul Avis (ed.), 2011, *The Journey of Christian Initiation*, London: Church House Publishing.

11 C. O. Buchanan, forthcoming.

12 J. D. C. Fisher, 1975, *The Fullness of Christian Initiation*, Cowley, Oxford: Bocardo & Church Army Press.

13 P. de Clerke, 2012, 'The Confirmation of Baptism: A historico-theological interpretation, towards a renewed pastoral approach', in *Studia Liturgica* 42 (1–2), pp. 190–6.

14 A different version is provided in *Patterns for Worship* (1995) and a further variant in *Common Worship: Initiation Services* (1998).

15 K. Stevenson, 1981, *Family Services*, Alcuin Club Manual No. 3, London: Alcuin Club/SPCK.

16 Liturgical Commission, 1989, *Patterns for Worship*, GS 898, London: Church House Publishing.

17 Church of England, 1994, *A Service of the Word and Affirmations of Faith*, London: Church House Publishing; Church of England, 1995, *Patterns for Worship*, London: Church House Publishing.

18 Daniel Young, 1983, *Welcoming Children to Communion*, Grove Worship Series 85, Bramcote: Grove Books.

19 Board of Education Working Party, 1985, *Communion before Confirmation?* London: Church Information Office.

20 Board of Education, 1988, *Children in the Way*, London: National Society/Church House Publishing.

21 British Council of Churches, 1989, *Children and Holy Communion*, Shoreham: Design and Print. See also, D. G. Hamilton, and F. A. J. Macdonald, 1982, *Children at the Table*, Edinburgh: Dept of Education, Church of Scotland; United Reformed Church in England and Wales, 1988, *Children in Communion?* London: United Reformed Church.

22 B. Kay, J. Greenough and J. D. Gay, 1993, *Communion before Confirmation: A Report on the Survey Conducted by Culham College Institute*, Abingdon: Culham College Institute.

23 Church of England, 2012, *Additional Eucharistic Prayers: With Guidance on Celebrating the Eucharist with Children*, London: Church House Publishing. See also T. Stratford, and P. Tovey, 2012, *Introducing Additional Eucharistic Prayers*, Cambridge: Grove Books.

24 Stephen Lake, 2006, *Let the Children Come – to Communion*, London: SPCK.

25 C. O. Buchanan, 1974, *Baptismal Discipline*, Grove Worship Series 3, Bramcote: Grove Books.

26 C. O. Buchanan, 1973, 2009, *A Case for Infant Baptism*, Grove Worship Series 20, Bramcote: Grove Books.

27 C. O. Buchanan, 1993, *Infant Baptism and the Gospel*, London: Darton, Longman and Todd.

28 Mark Dalby, 1989, *Open Baptism*, London: SPCK.

29 Leslie J. Francis, Susan H. Jones and David W. Lankshear, 1996, 'Baptism Policy and Church Growth in Church of England Rural, Urban and Suburban Parishes' in *Modern Believing*, 37, No. 3, 11–24.

30 House of Bishops, 1992, 'Baptism and Fonts'.

31 S. Anita Stauffer, 1994, *On Baptismal Fonts: Ancient and Modern*, Nottingham: Grove Books.

8

On the Way to Common Worship: Mission in a Postmodern World

The Church of England continued to debate, through Synod motions, official reports and the writings of various people, different routes for baptismal candidates. This was background discussion for the further revising of the baptismal liturgy. Liturgical revision led to *Common Worship: Initiation Services* (1998).[1] This was not uniformly welcomed and changes of the rubrics, the addition of catechumenal material, and the addition of reconciliation rites, led to *Common Worship: Christian Initiation* (2006).[2] Even this has not satisfied people and new alternative texts, provided in response to the 2011 General Synod motion from Liverpool diocese for more accessibility in language, were hotly discussed in the press and in the Church in 2014.[3] All of this tends to suggest that baptism and mission will continue to be an ongoing issue. It is the lack of any common mind in the Church as a whole that leads to constant production of policy papers and suggestions for change within the mission context today.

How many routes?

The production of two papers from General Synod, with different ideas about Christian initiation, occurred in 1991. *Christian Initiation – A Policy for the Church of England* by Martin Reardon said that there were four options: the Eastern pattern of baptism and chrismation followed by communion; the traditional Anglican pattern of infant baptism, confirmation followed by communion; the modified Anglican pattern where confirmation might be performed at the age of seven followed by testimony as a public profession of faith; and the Ely proposal of admission to communion before confirmation with the rite of commissioning later in life.[4] The report argued for flexibility while admitting that four different patterns living side by side might be difficult to sustain.

The second paper for General Synod, *Christian Initiation and Its Relation to Some Pastoral Offices,* was written by Kenneth Stevenson and David Stancliffe.[5] This report noted the ongoing change of context and thus churches ranged from the 'missionary' to the 'folk church' with shades in between. It envisaged three routes to Christian faith and practice. Route 1 is the traditional one of infant baptism, confirmation and then communion. Route 2 is baptism, confirmation and Eucharist as an integral whole. The authors suggested that this presupposed candidates who could answer for themselves and is a 'church against the world' ecclesiology. Route 3 is those who need staged rites of various kinds which includes the lapsed, Christians transferring church membership, and those who need a rite of spiritual wholeness.

While these two papers overlap, and the second attends particularly to liturgical issues, which were to be included in the new baptismal rites, there is nonetheless a certain amount of divergence between them.

On the Way (1995)

This report is perhaps the most significant after the Ely report in a principal discussion of baptism for the Church of England.[6] The subtitle, *Towards an Integrated Approach to Christian Initiation* indicates the wider interest of the report setting baptism within the context of mission. Its starting point is adult initiation today and it looks at how people come to faith, drawing on the work of John Finney.[7] In suggesting 10 different issues in taking the initiation of adults into account, two here are of particular importance: 'Christian initiation should integrate, living and believing, and enable people to assimilate usable patterns of worship, faith and life'; also, 'the links between baptism and evangelism, and between baptism and Christian living, need to be recovered'. With this in mind the report encourages the adaptation of catechumenal approaches for adult initiation.

The report then sees four strands in pastoral strategy. The first strand is evangelism, where it notes a degree of conflict between the desire for pastoral care (and evangelism) and the historic commitment of the Church of England to pastoral care of the whole nation. The second strand is that of education, where it sees the need for further education of the people of God. This was also identified in the Ely report. However, the report at this point features quite a wide discussion, not least including the place of church schools in Christian education. In many parts of the world church schools have been a substantial tool in mission and bringing people to faith. The report looks to a greater partnership between school and church. The third strand is liturgy, where it notes that church life is increasingly bewildering to those outside. The report does not fully endorse the idea that worship should be increasingly accessible and all elements that are alien to that should be abandoned. Rather it bemoans the lack in many parishes of a bridging environment in which people can explore aspects of Christian worship. It sees catechumenal approaches as valuable here. The fourth strand is ethics, where the report notes the ethical exhortations in the Scriptures and the need of ethical formation of new Christians.

After this discussion the initiation of children is considered. Possible catechumenal approaches are discussed, but the enrolment of infants as enquirers is not suggested as a route, although this might be appropriate for some parents. It then begins to question some of the assumptions of the ASB, noting the tone of the rite lacks welcome and that the question of parental faith is complex. It notes that the changing society and church relationship continues to fuel ongoing discussion.

This was a major report on the place of baptism in society today and its relationship with the evangelism and mission of the Church. It is rather unfortunate that it was not fully debated. The chair made clear that the work was primarily done by Michael Vasey, whose untimely death removed one of the key advocates of the report. However many of the suggestions were to be included in *Common Worship: Christian Initiation*.

Mission in theory and practice

The Church of England has been debating mission to the nation continually. In the post-war period this included *Towards the Conversion of England* (1945), *The Marks of Mission* (1984), *Building Missionary Congregations* (1996) and more recently *Mission-shaped Church* (2004), to name a few.[8] *The Marks of Mission* developed by the Anglican Consultative Council was an inter-Anglican document. The second mark is to 'teach, baptize and nurture new believers' thus making baptism central to mission. More disappointing in this area, perhaps, is *Mission-shaped Church,* in which baptism gets only a passing reference and the marks of mission seem to have been forgotten. However, in *Building Missionary Congregations* Robert Warren recognized the need 'to recover the baptismal identity of every believer'. He identifies the danger of Christianity being a bolt-on to a prevailing secular lifestyle and wishes to thoroughly Christianize believers. In this he sees as necessary greater exploration and integration of Christian faith into a person's lifestyle such that people may see Christians and question what their faith is about because of the hope that is in them. He thus supports catechumenal approaches of nurture, as the approach tries to integrate the baptismal identity with beliefs and practice including worship.

Parallel to this one might see the call for a renewal of baptismal spirituality in the work of Maxwell Johnson, as giving some indication of the development of baptismal identity and the shape that might hold.[9] He has eight elements to this baptismal spirituality. The first is to reclaim the radical equalization of baptism. Baptism leads us into a radical multicultural worldwide Church and provides a baptismal unity within this diverse body. This view challenges our narrow parochialism and our traditional views of roles and structures. His second element is that we should re-evaluate the relationship between baptism and confirmation. Johnson believes that the reuniting of baptism and confirmation needs to occur not only in adult initiation but in all initiation. This might challenge the traditional role of the bishop within Anglicanism. His third element is to advocate the practice of the communion of all the baptized. Making secondary rites a prerequisite to communion undermines baptism and marginalizes a group (often children) within the congregation. Fourth, he wishes we be aware of creeping Pelagianism. Emphasizing that God's gracious gift in the font needs to be put over against our decision or the implementation of fences to be jumped over. Fifth he wants a renewed sense of baptismal focus at the centre of the liturgical year. Many churches still do not have an Easter Vigil and even fewer have baptisms at it. Baptismal spirituality might suggest that the opportunity is taken for parts of the Christian year to emphasize baptism. Sixth, he wants a new sense of ministry. In baptism we become part of the royal priesthood; all are therefore called to work as part of the body of Christ in the world. It is not the part of the ordained to do the mission and the laity to be passive. All are involved in many and various ways. Seventh, Johnson wants a new ecumenical zeal: one Lord, one Church, one baptism; baptism should drive ecumenism. Eighth, and finally, he wishes to see a renewed sense of all Christian life being a living out of baptism. A deeper understanding of the implications of being baptized needs to flow through everyone in our congregations. In particular the last two should have significant mission implications.

Perhaps the most well-known outreach course has become the Alpha Course.[10] This began in the 1970s and was developed when Nicky Gumbel took over the course in 1990. In 1993 the first Alpha conference was held to show how others could use the course. Since then it has become a worldwide movement. Alpha has its own rituals, a meal, worship, teaching and a discussion and a particularly charismatic focus on healing and the weekend devoted to the Holy Spirit. Some see this as a particular expression of John Wimber's *Power Evangelism*.[11] It is however a significant factor in evangelization in the Church.

Other courses have integrated more with official Church of England provision. The Emmaus course used services from *Rites on the Way*, even before they were fully approved and thus enabled them to be road-tested alongside a nurture course.[12] The Pilgrim course uses the questions and the decision from *Common Worship* as part of its design. It integrates the 'Rites Approaching Baptism' of *Common Worship* into its programme and uses the traditional catechetical foci of the Lord's Prayer, the ten Commandments, the beatitudes and the creed as part of its content.[13]

The purpose here is not to review every method of evangelism in Christian nurture, but to indicate that alongside liturgical renewal has gone, hand-in-hand, the development of practical courses for parishes to run. The materials are there, the question is about the zeal of parishes to use them. In one area however there continues to be a weakness, and that is in a provision for a catechetical lectionary. In the past there was a tradition of preaching through the catechism. This could easily apply to the Lord's Prayer, the ten Commandments and the beatitudes, all of which are biblical material. There is also a tradition of preaching through the Apostles' Creed. Lectionary material under the provision of 'open season lectionary' in these particular areas would strengthen nurture, and alongside small-group work could be used in teaching for the rest of the Church.

Common Worship – baptismal rites

Common Worship: Initiation Services came out in 1998. This was an interim piece of work because at the same time *Rites on the Way* was going through General Synod.[14] These were various catechumenal rites that were being developed in light of *On the Way*. They were revised and incorporated into *Common Worship: Christian Initiation* (2006). The aim of the rest of the chapter is to examine the contents of *Christian Initiation* in light of the previous discussion. The section that will be omitted is recovering baptism with its service of penitence, reconciliation and wholeness and healing. These are more than adequately considered elsewhere.[15]

Rites on the way: approaching baptism

This section begins with 'Thanksgiving for the Gift of a Child'. We have seen that this was one positive outcome of the Ely discussion, which had gone alongside the doctrine commission's report on this service. The service includes thanksgiving and blessing (previously blessing was regarded as inappropriate in this service) and the giving of the gospel to the family as their guide. There are alternative prayers that may be used by the child who has been adopted. While this is still not catechumenal it may in practice be used in that way, particularly as the suggested texts, 'rites and forms of prayer supporting the baptism of infants' were mostly omitted from the final revision but were mildly catechumenal for infant baptism.

The second part of this first section is of 'rites supporting disciples on the way of Christ'. This is in two parts; one is for the baptism of children, and the other for the baptism of adults. The welcome of those preparing for the baptism of children is a pastoral rite of introduction to the congregation and prayer, and is the one part of what would have been a richer provision in support of infant baptism. The other rites in this section support the baptism of adults. None of these are compulsory and can easily be adapted but may provide helpful stages for people within their journey towards baptism. They are assumed to be parallel to nurture groups within the church and call for congregational involvement in the process, not only in terms of becoming sponsors, but also in terms of a conscious congregational participation in the process. The inclusion of these rites into the Church of England argues against Christian nurture being something done by clergy outside congregational participation. It is the fruition of a long discussion about the catechumenate and the need for greater provision for adult baptism in a missional context.

Baptism and confirmation

This section of *Common Worship* is complex, reflecting the multiplicity of views within the Church of England. There are five main parts:

1. Holy baptism – where the archetypal rite is baptism within Holy Communion (and then directions when it is not).
2. Emergency baptism.
3. Holy baptism and confirmation – now a derivative rite, and its alternatives of being without Holy Communion and at vigil services.
4. Seasonal provisions.
5. Supplementary texts.

The provision has one archetypal service, Baptism with Holy Communion. Here the service moves from the liturgy of the word, to the liturgy of baptism and then to the liturgy of the Eucharist, without any mention of confirmation. This gives the impression that both adults and infants may be admitted to and receive Holy Communion without confirmation at all. The second derivative service is of baptism and confirmation and Holy Communion. This is the type of unified rite that the Church of England has been producing in line with the 1958 report *Baptism and Confirmation*. *Common Worship* initiation seems to have moved beyond the 1958 report.

It is quite clear that the preference is for baptism to be within a service of Holy Communion, whatever the age of the candidates. This is shown by what is not included, that is, a service of infant baptism which is easily usable in the context of an afternoon service. In this sense it moves further than the ASB, where there was a service of infant baptism, which was widely used in afternoon services, and *Common Worship* leaves ministers to work out and develop such a rite themselves.

At this point some detailed comments on parts of the service might be appropriate. There is a strengthening of words of welcome within the service indicating the need and providing a possible text, the introduction. This is in part a response to the perceived lack of welcome of the ASB text.

The decision changes the ASB approach. Not only is this now a set of six questions, designed to enhance this section of the service, but actually the way faith is articulated is changed. The rubric says that the candidates are addressed directly, or in the case of a child they are directly addressed through their parents and godparents. So you no longer answer 'for yourself and for this child' but answer on behalf of the child. This is a return to a more prayer book way of seeing faith articulated. Within the decision the first question asks for a rejection of the devil, which again is a departure from the ASB where you are only asked to reject evil, and where rejection of evil occurs after turning to Christ. In practice the questions have proven overly strong and often there is a sense of heaviness at this point, so the rubrics now allow the inclusion of the ASB form instead of this text. Indeed there is the possibility of further variations at this point.

The signing with the cross continues in the ASB position, as a completion of the decision. The notes say that this may include oil, the oil of catechumens, but a new development is that parents and godparents may also be involved in making the sign of the cross after the minister. In practice this can work quite well and feel an inclusive activity for the supporters.

The prayer over the water is supplemented by seasonal provisions for three baptismal seasons, Epiphany/Baptism of Christ/Trinity, Easter/Pentecost, and all Saints. Each season includes a full provision of material including introductions, blessing of the light, collects, Bible reading and psalms, prayer over the water, intercessions, introduction to the peace, prefaces, post communion prayers, and blessing. This could potentially lead to a significant baptismal consciousness of the congregation, if used.

The profession of faith is again expressed in a new way. The candidates are asked to profess their faith in an interrogatory version of the Apostles' Creed. This is done with the congregation, expressing that the faith is not simply of the candidate, or of the family, but is the faith of the Church. Again, for those who preferred the ASB, the questions from that book can be found in an appendix.

Post-baptismal ceremonies include the clothing with a white robe as an option. This is partially with a view to the service including adults. The compulsory prayer after baptism for the pouring out of grace and a daily anointing by the Spirit on the candidate may be accompanied with chrism. For those who hold a more Orthodox approach to baptism the candidates would then be fully initiated, whatever their age, and receive the Eucharist.

The commission includes alternative versions for infant baptism and for adult baptism. Here the duties of candidates are spelled out, including the need to come for confirmation for infants. Bryan Spinks has noted a welcome departure from the ASB here.[16] His sees the setting up of demands before baptism as undermining baptism as a free gift of grace. Here the grace of baptism is received and then the demands of discipleship are presented. It is through baptism that we can fulfil the demands of the gospel. Baptism enables us to be holy, rather than we have to be holy in order to be baptized.

The giving of the lighted candle is placed between the blessing and the dismissal (although it may occur immediately after baptism). This is a deliberate missional changing of the liturgy. The candidate is now to go as a light in the world. It is not about personal development and self-improvement, but about the missionary nature of baptism and of the candidate's baptismal life.

A second service is of holy baptism and confirmation. This has its own variations although there is no obvious reason as to why the greeting in this service is different, apart from perhaps the bishop being present. Distinctive to this rite is the rubric which disallows chrism at the post-baptismal prayer if chrism is allowed at the confirmation. Rubrics allow the inclusion of affirmation and reception in this service. The service of reception is for people who are transferring from another denomination to the Church of England. The service of affirmation is for someone who may have gone through all types of baptismal rite (baptism and confirmation) but come to a lively faith and wish to express that renewal in a public service. Neither of these services has to be led by a bishop.

The confirmation itself is quite short, versicles and responses, the confirmation prayer for the Spirit, and a hand laying, which may involve the use of chrism. As affirmation and reception are included in the service the traditional prayer 'Defend O Lord' becomes a congregational prayer for all the candidates.

Rites of affirmation: appropriating baptism

This section includes six different services. In some contexts parishes go to a celebration of baptism and confirmation in the Cathedral, or as a deanery service. In this case there are some prayers and a welcome for candidates to whom this has happened. This is to reincorporate them into the congregation. They are then incorporated in the next service where a 'thanksgiving for holy baptism' occurs within the main service bringing together the congregation and the newly baptized in a common framework.

'The admission of the baptized to communion' is something rather different. This is liturgical material for those who are admitted to communion before confirmation. As such it expresses the alternative pattern of initiation approved by the Church of England, and suggested by the Ely report.

A form for the corporate renewal of baptismal vows is included and it is suggested that this become a regular part of congregational life. They may be used in baptismal seasons of Easter, Pentecost, and the baptism of Christ (the first Sunday of Epiphany). They are also appropriate at the inauguration of a new ministry. Sprinkling with water from the font or signing oneself with water from the font are seen as appropriate actions. Parishes would need to think through how they might heighten their baptismal spirituality and incorporate this rite within that initiative.

Two services are now included, affirmation and reception. The first service could be used in a variety of pastoral contexts, one being the coming to faith of somebody who has already been baptized and confirmed, the other being for an active Christian who has lapsed. While this may be incorporated into the service of baptism and confirmation, it can also be used separately as a stand-alone service and, unlike many other Provinces, the Church of England does not require this to be done by the bishop. The candidates are presented and questioned to make sure that they have already been baptized. Then they recommit themselves to the decisions made at baptism. They profess their faith with the congregation in the interrogatory creed. They publicly renew a commitment to Jesus Christ and may go to the font to sign themselves with water. The prayer of affirmation follows the structure of confirmation; a prayer for the candidate with hands extended, the laying on of a hand for each candidate with appropriate words, and a congregational prayer using 'Defend O Lord'. This is followed by a commissioning, intercessions and the Eucharist. This type of service was envisioned at the Inter Anglican Liturgical Consultation in Toronto, and has been developed in a number of Provinces of the Anglican Communion. Its bolder use in parishes might be of great strengthening to the Church.

The second service is that of reception into communion of the Church of England. This service may now be presided over by the parish priest, unless the actual candidate is a priest wherein the service needs to be led by the bishop. Like in the affirmation service at the presentation candidates are asked if they had been baptized. The decision may be omitted otherwise it follows the standard baptismal form. The profession of faith is the usual interrogatory creed. The declaration asks questions about the Church of England as part of the one holy catholic and apostolic Church, the willingness of the candidate to accept its teaching and discipline, and the commitment of the candidate to take part in the worship and mission of the Church. The reception itself again follows the structure of confirmation. A prayer is said with hands outstretched towards the candidate, but then the person is received into the Church with the right hand of fellowship. The prayer 'Defend O Lord' is used as a congregational prayer for the person received.

The Notes refer to Canon B28 which distinguishes between three categories: first those who are unbaptized or invalidly baptized, who need baptism as reception into the Church of England;

second those who are baptized but not episcopally confirmed, who should be confirmed (although it is not quite clear what this means in terms of someone in the Porvoo Communion)[17]; and third those who have been episcopally confirmed or received unction who may use the rite of reception. This canon creaks significantly in the light of increasing ecumenical cooperation and the acknowledgement of baptism as the basis of joining the Church. The Ely report asked that confirmation cease to be used as a rite of transfer. In an increasingly complex global society these simple categories developed by this canon look increasingly thin. We are already in a full Communion relationship with a series of Lutheran churches, the Porvoo Communion, but most of the people on the Lutheran side of that Communion will not have been episcopally confirmed, but presbyterally confirmed. From another perspective it is quite possible that people may have been episcopally confirmed in other Protestant churches, for example, Moravians or some forms of Methodism, but presumably at this point there will be a qualification of 'episcopally confirmed' requiring the bishop to be in historic episcopate. That could become quite complex with the Moravians, as Anglican bishops have already participated in episcopal consecrations, and there is a full Communion agreement with the Episcopal Church. There are clearly complex ecumenical issues that need to be thought through, but these are linked to the underlying issue of the relationship of baptism and confirmation and the failure of the Church of England to grasp the nettle.

Commentary

Both editions of the *Common Worship* initiation services include a commentary by the Liturgical Commission. These differ significantly from one another and both are worth reading. *Christian Initiation* clearly has more services to comment on than *Initiation Services*. However, *Initiation Services* seems to acknowledge more clearly the diversity that the Liturgical Commission has had to cope with, and the incomplete nature of the rites. *Christian*

Initiation seems more concerned to give the right answer to difficult questions. Thus the use of chrism at baptism, affirmation and reception is simply denied as equivalent to confirmation. This would seem to be in conflict with Orthodox believers being received into the Church without the requirement of confirmation, one of a number of points where the commentaries vary. *Christian Initiation* concludes with a thanksgiving for the life of Michael Vasey and an acknowledgement of his significant contribution to the work of developing a liturgy appropriate for the mission of the church today.

Postscript

This book has looked at baptism and mission from Jesus to *Common Worship*. The last few chapters have concentrated on the situation of the Church of England, and the issues are replicated in other churches of the West. While this book is being written Synod is dealing with more alternatives within the baptismal liturgy. The instability of the rite is due in part to a lack of common mind within the Church in terms both of the meaning of baptism and of the nature of mission today. We are however resourced with considerable liturgical material for the mission of the Church.

Notes

1 Church of England, 1997, *Common Worship: Initiation Services*, London: Church House Publishing.

2 Church of England, 2006, *Common Worship: Christian Initiation*, London: Church House Publishing.

3 General Synod, 2011, *Liverpool Diocesan Synod Motion Common Worship Baptism Provision*, GS 1816a, London: General Synod.

4 M. A. Reardon, 1991, *Christian Initiation: A Policy for the Church of England: A Discussion Paper*, GS Misc. 635, London: Church House Publishing.

5 K. Stevenson and D. Stancliffe, 1991, *Christian Initiation and Its Relation to Some Pastoral Offices: A Paper Prepared on Behalf of the Liturgical Commission*, GS Misc. 366, London: General Synod of the Church of England.

6 General Synod, 1995, *On the Way: Towards an Integrated Approach to Christian Initiation*, GS Misc. 444, London: Church House Publishing.

7 J. Finney, 1992, *Finding Faith Today: How does it happen?* Swindon: Bible Society.

8 Archbishop's Commission on Evangelism, 1945, *Towards the Conversion of England*, Westminster: Press and Publications Board of the Church Assembly; Church of England, *The Five Marks of Mission*, www.churchofengland.org/media/1918854/the%20five%20marks%20of%20mission.pdf (accessed 2015); Robert Warren, 1995, *Building Missionary Congregations: Towards a Post-Modern Way of Being Church*, London: Church House Publishing; Mission and Public Affairs Council, 2004, *Mission-Shaped Church: Church Planting and Fresh Expressions of Church in a Changing Context*, London: Church House Publishing.

9 Maxwell E. Johnson, 1999, *The Rites of Christian Initiation: Their Evolution and Interpretation,* Collegeville: Liturgical Press.

10 N. Gumbel, 1996, *Alpha Course Manual*, London: HTB Publications.

11 John Wimber and Kevin Springer, 1986, *Power Evangelism*, San Francisco: Harper & Row.

12 Stephen Cottrell, 2003, *Emmaus: The Way of Faith*, London: Church House Publishing.

13 Stephen Cottrell, 2013, *Pilgrim: A Course for the Christian Journey*, London: Church House Publishing.

14 Liturgical Commission, 1998, *Rites on the Way: Work in Progress*, GS Misc. 530, London: General Synod.

15 Phillip Tovey, (ed), 2006, *Common Worship Reconciliation and Restoration; A Commentary*, Grove Worship Series 187, Cambridge: Grove Books.

16 Bryan D. Spinks, 2002, 'Cranmer, Baptism and Christian Nurture; or Totonto Revisited', in *Studia Liturgica* 32, No. 1: 98–110.

17 Nordic Lutherans and British Isle Anglicans signed a full communion agreement at Porvoo in Finland in 1992.

9

Final Thoughts

This chapter is not so much a conclusion as some final thoughts. I hope by now you are coming to your own conclusions and considering baptism and mission in your local context. This is not a book to tell you practically how that should be done and these final thoughts are not here to solve all problems both in the Church of England and local churches. This book has, however, tried to show a close link between baptism and mission. If the Church is involved in mission then it will be baptizing. Indeed the Church is involved in mission as a baptismal community, for in baptism we see the fruit of mission, and a call to mission. For baptism is an effectual sign of the grace of God revealed to us in Jesus Christ and applied to us by the Holy Spirit.[1] Thus the preaching of the gospel and baptism talk the same language: that of Jesus Christ. This chapter instead looks at some wider issues behind local discussion.

The Anglican Communion

The 1968 Lambeth Conference encouraged each Province to explore the theology of baptism and confirmation and to experiment in this regard. It is now time to reflect on progress.[2] There would appear to have been four different approaches to this resolution.

First, there are Provinces which continue to follow the pattern of the Book of Common Prayer, that is, baptism followed by confirmation which is a prerequisite to receiving communion. In this category could be seen the churches in, for example, Uganda,

Tanzania, the Indian Ocean, southeast Asia, the South Cone. This is not an exhaustive list, but there is a large part of the Communion that has yet to even begin any exploration of anything but the inherited pattern.

Second, there are those who have wholeheartedly taken on the view that baptism is full sacramental initiation and the only prerequisite to receiving communion. In this category are Provinces such as the Episcopal Church (in the United States of America), the Anglican Church of Canada, the Episcopal Church of Scotland, the Anglican Church of Kenya, and the Anglican Church in Aotearoa, New Zealand and Polynesia. Again this is not a full list; indeed one of the things needed is a complete review within the Anglican Communion. In Provinces taking this view children are baptized and may be later admitted to communion (though not by confirmation); adults are baptized and thereby immediately admitted to communion. Confirmation becomes a later rite of commitment and commissioning to mission.

Third, there are those Provinces which have a mixed economy. The Church of England represents this with the norm being the traditional pattern but parishes being able to petition the bishop for the second pattern. The chapters above have tracked the development of this approach in the Church.

The final pattern is an ecumenical one, which can be seen in the Church of South India and the Church of North India. In both these churches there are two routes of initiation: one through infant baptism and the other through believer's baptism; both come together in confirmation. This is an older ecumenically forged pattern where the inclusion of Baptists and other believer baptism churches led to the inclusion of both patterns into the new Church. Congregations will tend to follow either pattern depending on their history. However, what this makes of confirmation after believer's baptism is not clear. This approach is ecumenically useful but does not solve the question as to why confirmation is needed before communion when someone has professed faith at baptism. Nor does this approach come to grips with new exploration of the theology of baptism seeing it as complete sacramental initiation.

Clearly the Anglican Communion moves at different speeds. The liturgists of the Communion have advocated the second pattern as was shown at the Toronto meeting of the IALC. It is likely that there will be a gradual move towards the second pattern as children once admitted to communion are not supposed to be excommunicated when they move church or Province. However, at the same time there has been an increase in confirmation in New Zealand from people who have migrated there and are used to the traditional approach.[3]

Mission

Baptismal renewal and renewal of mission need to go together. Just as the Church needs to see itself as a baptizing community, so it needs to see itself as a Church in mission. In order to do this, both baptism and mission must not be seen as the job of the clergy, but the work of the whole Church. It is how the whole Church participates in the mission of God.

For some traditional churches this may seem quite scary. Mission and particularly evangelism may be seen as street preaching and knocking on doors, something which people find quite unattractive. Studies would seem to show that effective ways of mission are through small discussion groups, something that churches have skills in and knowledge how to develop.[4] Each parish needs to be running enquirers groups as a regular feature of their life, and this should not be the work of the minister but a shared effort of the congregation. This can be shared by people offering both the venue and food. The leading can be shared, indeed it could be completely lay-led, and Readers could have a particular function here. It can also be shared with the congregation in their prayers. When people have progressed and wish to be baptized they can be introduced to the congregation, and regularly prayed for through the baptismal process. This type of joint work needs to be locally adapted according to practicalities. However the aim is to express the ministry of the baptizing community.[5] The minister will have a part in this process but will not dominate it. Baptism is not just the job of the minister but of the whole church.

On the Way pointed out that schools in particular play an important role, not least because the Church of England has a considerable number of them and part of its mission is the education of people.[6] However there is also an opportunity for Christian assemblies and other groups, and help in religious education. This needs to be a key part of the mission of a parish where there is a church school. Mission in the past here and overseas made schools a key part of the strategy, Christian education leading to Christian practice. This fed into youth work and baptism and confirmation groups.

Baptismal ecclesiology has been developing over a number of years. Too often liturgical renewal has led to a gathered and inward looking church. Baptism is not about joining a club, but responding to Jesus. We need a baptismal ecclesiology that looks outward and connects to society, not runs away from it.[7]

As previously mentioned part of the requirement for renewal in mission is to develop a stronger baptismal spirituality.[8] This includes the way we view other Christians and there is need to continue to work at the ecumenical movement both internationally and locally in order to remove the stumbling block of division. However, there are many other things that can be done to strengthen our baptismal spirituality and these have been touched upon in chapters above. The renewal of baptismal vows at key seasons such as the Baptism of Christ, Easter, Pentecost, and All Saints might be a start in the right direction. Richard Giles rightly comments that Sunday worship continues by and large to ignore the font.[9] The penny needs to drop that the font is not a once in a lifetime place but a continual centre for renewal. We need to think creatively to show the font as the focus of unity and mission.

Liturgy

In England it is unlikely that we have reached a stable position with regard to baptism. The number of parishes admitting the baptized to communion continues to grow, and this in turn challenges other parishes as people migrate from one parish to another. In the end a more fully committed position needs to be arrived at and put into practice, rather than a rather grudging allowance of an 'alternative' route. It would be much better if it was said that there are two routes both fully accepted by the Church of England. To do this may require some changes of the canons.

Ecumenically, the Ely report questioned the use of confirmation as a rite of transfer. Today if a Baptist or Methodist transfers to the Church of England they do this by being confirmed. We have already seen that there is difficulty in this with regard to the Porvoo Communion. The problem is that confirmation is being regarded as prerequisite to receiving Holy Communion. The focus needs to be directed instead to baptism for, if it is accepted as complete sacramental initiation, all that is then needed is the reception into the Church of England for those who are baptized. In churches where there are covenant relationships, for example with Methodists, which is at a denominational level, this would be a significant step forward.

There needs to be rethinking about children and families that come for baptism but seem to have little connection with church. Mission suggests that a warm welcome needs to be provided and alongside that we need good processes that lead people forward in faith from one level of practice to a deeper level of praxis.[10] This was begun in *Rites on the Way* but only at a superficial level.[11] The draft versions had included an American model of catechumenal type of approaches for parents who bring children for baptism, and it appears that this was unacceptable as these were dropped out of further revisions of the report, so what is needed is to develop something more appropriate for the Church of England.[12] Unless this is done some parishes will continue to using thanksgivings as a way to avoid infant baptism. Something that begins a catechumenal process is needed both for the child and for the family. The danger is that the opportunity of an open door is missed.

The other aspect that should not be neglected is that of architecture. Baptismal renewal may require a look at our architectural symbolism, which in some places negates the importance of baptism. There has been a trend for the introduction of baptisteries and it is unlikely that this will diminish, for there are an increasing number of adult baptisms. But there are some significant examples of the re-positioning of fonts giving them an importance within the building suitable for the sacrament of baptism. As churches are reordered or restored so careful thinking needs to go into this area.[13]

The encouragement of Lambeth 68 needs to be taken up wholeheartedly within the Communion. The five marks of mission include baptism as a part of our missional life. As we renew our mission so we need to renew our theology and practice of baptism, for they are one in the mission of God in Jesus Christ.

Notes

1 See Article 25.

2 Lambeth Conference, 1968, *The Lambeth Conference 1968: Resolutions and Reports*, London: SPCK.

3 B. Dawson and K. Dawson, 2009, *Here and Now: Confirmation in Tikanga Pakeha*, www.anglican.org.nz/Resources/Lectionary-and-Worship/Writing-on-Liturgy-from-this-Church (accessed, January 2015).

4 E.g., B. Jackson, 2002, *Hope for the Church*, London: Church House Publishing.

5 See A. Theodore Eastman, 1982, *The Baptizing Community: Christian Initiation and the Local Congregation*, New York: Seabury Press; P. Ball and M. Grundy, 2000, *Faith on the Way: A Practical Parish Guide to the Adult Catechumenate,* London: Mowbray.

6 General Synod, 1995, *On the Way: Towards an integrated approach to Christian Initiation*, GS Misc. 444, London: Church House Publishing.

7 See J. Dawson, 2011, *A Radical Theology of Baptism,* Porirua: Jenny Dawson.

8 Maxwell E. Johnson, 1999, *The Rites of Christian Initiation: Their Evolution and Interpretation*, Collegeville: Liturgical Press.

9 Richard Giles, 2008, *Times and Seasons: Creating transformative worship throughout the year*, New York: Church Publishing.

10 See A. Gilchrist, 2004, *Creating a Culture of Welcome*, Grove Evangelism Series 66, Cambridge: Grove Books.

11 Liturgical Commission, 1998, *Rites on the Way: Work in Progress*, GS Misc. 530, London: General Synod.

12 For the USA, see R. Meyers, 1997, *Continuing the Reformation: Re-Visioning Baptism in the Episcopal Church*, New York: Church Publishing.

13 S. Anita Stauffer, 1994, *On Baptismal Fonts: Ancient and Modern*, Nottingham: Grove Books.

Bibliography

The following bibliography is a survey of some of the more important works, and bibliographies within them should be consulted for further study. There is also an eye in this bibliography to works referred to in the text to enable further exploration.

Major academic works

There are two works which particularly are outstanding on rites of baptism. One is M. E. Johnson, 1999, *The Rites of Christian Initiation: Their evolution and interpretation*, Collegeville: Liturgical Press. This is a comprehensive study of rites of baptism with an excellent bibliography bringing together much of the thinking of recent years. The other is the two volumes by one author: B. D. Spinks, 2006, *Early and Medieval Rituals and Theologies of Baptism: From the New Testament to the Council of Trent*, Aldershot: Ashgate, and B. D. Spinks, 2006, *Reformation and Modern Rituals and Theologies of Baptism: From Luther to Contemporary Practices*, Aldershot: Ashgate. Once again there is a thoroughly scholarly discussion of baptismal liturgy. These works are of a more academic nature, possibly aimed at postgraduate studies.

For some more specialized areas

Of continued importance propounding the theory behind much modern baptismal revision is J. D. C. Fisher, 1965, *Christian*

Initiation: Baptism in the Medieval West, Alcuin Club Collection 47, London: SPCK. A more specialized study of the Victorian period is P. J. Jagger, 1982, *Clouded Witness: Initiation in the Church of England in the Mid-Victorian period, 1850–1875*, Allison Park: Pickwick Publications. Some of the conclusions of Jagger's work are modified by P. Tovey, 2014, *Anglican Confirmation: 1662–1820*, Farnham: Ashgate, which has much material on this neglected period. The classic work demolishing Dix's theory is G. W. H. Lampe, 1967, *The Seal of the Spirit: A study in the Doctrine of Baptism and Confirmation in the New Testament and the Fathers*, 2nd edn, London: SPCK.

A work looking at classical Anglican views is K. W. Stevenson, 1998, *The Mystery of Baptism in the Anglican Tradition*, Norwich: Canterbury Press. An important work detailing changes in the Episcopal Church in America is R. A. Meyers, 1997, *Continuing the Reformation: Re-visioning Baptism in the Episcopal Church*, New York: Church Publishing. Of particular importance within the Anglican Communion is D. Holeton (ed.), 1993, *Growing in Newness of Life: Christian Initiation in Anglicanism today: Papers from the Fourth International Anglican Liturgical Consultation, Toronto, 1991*, Anglican Book Centre: Toronto.

Baptismal texts

There are various collections of baptismal texts. Whitaker's 1960 book has recently been revised: E. C. Whitaker and Maxwell E. Johnson, 2003, *Documents of the Baptismal Liturgy*, Collegeville: Liturgical Press. The Baptism, Eucharist and Ministry process led to the production of a book which includes present baptismal rites: M. Thurian and G. Wainwright, 1983, *Baptism and Eucharist: Ecumenical convergence in celebration*, Geneva: World Council of Churches Grand Rapids: Eerdmans. This has been further supplemented by another book containing texts: T. F. Best, 2008, *Baptism Today: Understanding, practice, ecumenical implications*, Collegeville: Liturgical Press. A helpful book will be the forthcoming collection of current Anglican texts: P. Tovey, *Current Anglican Baptismal Liturgies*, Canterbury Press.

Church of England reports

The Church of England has produced many reports in the post-war period. Of particular importance is the Ely report: Commission on Christian Initiation, 1971, *Christian Initiation: Birth and Growth in the Christian Society*, GS 30, London: Church Information Office. This is still worth studying and pondering on its partial implementation. The question of children was followed up by the Knaresborough report: Board of Education Working Party, 1985, *Communion before Confirmation?* London: CIO, and a general discussion of the place of children in the church: Board of Education, 1988, *Children in the Way*, London: National Society and Church House Publishing. Produced mostly by Michael Vasey the last report significantly puts initiation and mission together: General Synod, 1995, *On the Way: Towards an integrated approach to Christian Initiation*, GS Misc. 444, London: Church House Publishing. Finally, P. Avis, (ed.), 2011, *The Journey of Christian Initiation*, London: Church House Publishing, which was completely refuted by C. Buchanan, 2014, *Baptism as Complete Sacramental Initiation*, Grove Worship Series 219, Cambridge: Grove Books.

Works by Colin Buchanan

Colin Buchanan has produced numerous publications on baptism with a particular approach that he has consistently expounded. Perhaps the three most significant are: C. O. Buchanan, 1973, 2009, *A Case for Infant Baptism*, Grove Worship Series 20, Bramcote: Grove Books, which gives a particular approach to infant baptism; C. O. Buchanan, 1986, *Anglican Confirmation*, Grove Liturgical Study No. 48, Bramcote: Grove Books, which denounces any two-stage approaches; C. O. Buchanan, 1993, *Infant Baptism and the Gospel*, London: Darton, Longman and Todd, looks much broader at the historical debates.

Commentaries on *Common Worship*

Liturgical commentary is a genre alive and well in the Church of England with an overview of *Common Worship* in S. Jones and P. Tovey, 2001, 'Initiation Services', in *A Companion to Common Worship Volume 1*, P. Bradshaw (ed.), SPCK: London, pp. 48–178. Buchanan focuses in one particular area in C.O. Buchanan, 2001, *Infant Baptism in Common Worship*, Grove Worship Series 163, Cambridge: Grove Books. A more practical book that should be in every parish is M. Earey, T. Lloyd and I. Tarrant, 2007, *Connecting with Baptism: A Practical Guide to Christian Initiation today*, London: Church House Publishing.

Baptismal architecture

An older book that sets the scene on baptismal architecture is J. G. Davies, 1962, *The Architectural Setting of Baptism*, London: Barrie and Rockliff. This was helpfully updated by S. A. Stauffer, 1994, *On Baptismal Fonts: Ancient and Modern*, Nottingham: Grove Books. Official policy documents are also important: House of Bishops, 1992, *The Provision of Fonts*, letter to all Diocesan Advisory Committees.

Ecumenical works

Of absolute importance in the ecumenical discussion is World Council of Churches, 1982, *Baptism, Eucharist and Ministry*, Faith and Order Paper 111, Geneva: World Council of Churches. This was responded to by many churches and there are collections of the responses. Of further interest from the World Council of Churches is, World Council of Churches, 2011, *One Baptism: Towards mutual recognition: A study text*, Faith and Order Paper 210, Geneva: World Council of Churches, which follows up the 1982 report.

Anglican Baptist dialogue is of particular importance. The official report is: Anglican Communion Office and Baptist World Alliance, 2005, *Conversations Around the World 2000–2005: The report of the international conversations between the Anglican Communion and the Baptist World Alliance*, London: Anglican Communion Office. But a very helpful discussion is found in the following paper: P. S. Fiddes, 2002, 'Baptism and the Process of Christian Initiation', in *Ecumenical Review*.

Baptism and Bible

The old classic on baptism and still not surpassed is, G. R. Beasley-Murray, 1962, *Baptism in the New Testament*, London: Macmillan; New York: St Martin's Press. This might be supplemented by, M. O. Fape, 1999, *Paul's Concept of Baptism and its Present Implications for Believers: Walking in the newness of life*, Lewiston: E. Mellen Press. The other hammer in the Dix coffin was J. D. G. Dunn, 1970, *Baptism in the Holy Spirit: A re-examination of the New Testament teaching on the Gift of the Spirit in relation to Pentecostalism today*, Naperville: A. R. Allenson.

Orthodox and Oriental perspectives

Of continuing significance is the work on Orthodox and Oriental rites. A classic on the Byzantine rite is A. Schmemann, 1974, *Of Water and the Spirit: A liturgical study of baptism*, Crestwood: St. Vladimir's Seminary Press. The Syrian rites are also of importance. One of the most helpful ways into this is S. P. Brock, 1979, *The Holy Spirit in the Syrian Baptismal Tradition*, The Syrian

Churches Series Vol. 9, Poona: Anita Printers. There is also a useful commentary on the Syrian text: P. Tovey, 1993, *Spiritual and Celestial Mysteries*, Kunnamkulam: St Thomas Press.

Catechumenate

Peter Ball has been a keen advocate of modern catechetical approaches in a series of publications including: P. Ball, 1988, *Adult Believing: A guide to the Christian Initiation of adults*, New York: Paulist Press, and more recently, P. G. M. Ball, 2000, *Faith on the Way: A practical parish guide to the adult catechumenate*, London: Mowbray. There have been other advocates of the approach not least through Grove Books: M. Grundy, 1991, *Evangelization through the Adult Catechumenate*, Grove Booklets on Evangelism No. 15, Bramcote: Grove Books.

Patristic texts

Besides Whitaker's collection of early texts an important volume on preaching at baptism is E. Yarnold, 1972, *The Awe-inspiring Rites of Initiation: Baptismal homilies of the fourth century*, Slough: St Paul Publications. Then there are two important commentaries in the Hermenaia series: K. A. H. W. Niederwimmer, 1998, *The Didache: A commentary*, Minneapolis: Fortress Press and P. F. Bradshaw, Maxwell E. Johnson, and L. Edward Phillips, 2002, *The Apostolic Tradition: A commentary*, Minneapolis: Fortress Press. The latter is now the standard work on Hippolytus and if you use earlier work this must also be consulted.

Worship and mission

Questions of worship and mission were developed in J. G. Davies, 1967, *Worship and Mission*, New York: Association Press. A more recent approach from a radical reformation perspective is Alan Kreider and Eleanor Kreider, 2011, *Worship and Mission after Christendom*, Scottdale: Herald Press.

In England two books came out in the same year: C. Headley and M. Earey, 2002, *Mission and Liturgical Worship*, Grove Worship Series No. 170, Cambridge: Grove Books, and T. Stratford, 2002, *Liturgy and Urban Mission*, Grove Worship Series No. 173, Cambridge: Grove Books. These look at different aspects of worship and mission, the latter is particularly relevant to the Liverpool motion asking for further alternative baptismal texts. A recent book is R. Meyers, 2015, *Missional Worship, Worshipful Mission: Gathering as God's People, Going out in God's Name*, Grand Rapids: Eerdmans. Some of the ideas of this book occur in an article: P. Tovey, 2008, Models of Mission in Church of England Baptism Services, in *Anvil*, 25(3): pp. 209–11.

Children and communion

There are many books on children and communion, perhaps the standard text is now, S. Lake, 2006, *Let the Children come to Communion*, London: SPCK. There has been ongoing advocacy within Grove Books publications including D. Young, 1983, *Welcoming Children to Communion*, Grove Worship Series 85, Bramcote: Grove Books. See also, P. Reiss, 1998, *Children and Communion A Practical Guide for Interested Churches*, Grove Worship Series 149, Cambridge: Grove Books, and P. Reiss, 2015, *Infants and Children: Baptism and Communion*, Grove Worship Series 222, Cambridge: Grove Books.

A more historical look at children and communion is D. Holeton, 1981, *Infant Communion – Then and Now*, Grove Liturgical Study 27, Bramcote: Grove Books. Also, M. Dalby, 2003, *Infant Communion – the New Testament to the Reformation*, Joint Liturgical Study 56, Cambridge: Grove Books; M. Dalby, 2009, *Infant Communion Post-Reformation to Present Day*, Joint Liturgical Study 67, Norwich: Hymns Ancient and Modern and M. Dalby,

2013, *Admission to Communion: The Approaches of the Late Medievals and Reformers*, Joint Liturgical Study 75, Norwich: Hymns Ancient and Modern.

Two books that particularly study the views in the Anglican Communion are: R.A. Meyers, 1995, *Children at the Table: The communion of all the baptized in Anglicanism today*, New York: Church Hymnal Corporation, and C. O. Buchanan (ed.), 1985, *Nurturing Children in Communion: Essays from the Boston Consultation*, Grove Liturgical Study 44, Bramcote: Grove Books.

Index of Biblical Citations

Indexes compiled by Meg Davies
(Fellow of the Society of Indexers)

Index

Note: Page references in *italics* indicate tables.